Early praise for O

"*Penna & Phillips have done the world--the public and private sectors, corporations and individuals--a favor by compiling an important and very readable summary of the evolution of outcome thinking. Anyone whose desired goal is to select an outcome model for planning and evaluating programs will certainly get closer to that goal faster by reading this book. I couldn't imagine a more perfect summary about why and how to use outcome thinking.*"

Christopher M. Avery, Ph.D., President, Partnerworks
Author, Teamwork Is an Individual Skill: Getting Your
Work Done When Sharing Responsibility

"*All nonprofit organizations exist to achieve specific outcomes. Yet their leaders and managers often lack the tools to organize and assess progress in outcome terms--to the detriment of their clients and the effectiveness of the sector. Robert Penna and William Phillips' historical, conceptual, and very practical perspective on outcome-oriented management should be on the desk of every nonprofit CEO.*"

Paul Brest, President
The William and Flora Hewlett Foundation

"*With the multitude of papers and books addressing "outcome frameworks," it is easy to get lost in the woods... Penna and Phillips present a definitive overview of the field and provide the reader with an understandable review of the popular tools currently being applied in this rapidly changing field of practice.*"

Jed Emerson, Lecturer in Business
Stanford Business School

"*Outcome Frameworks breathes new life into essential ideas and practices that are too often misinterpreted as the narrow world of performance-based contracting*".

Robert Giloth, PhD.
Director of Family Economic Success
The Annie E. Casey Foundation

"An invaluable resource for those in the US and UK who are shifting from funder to investor. Building on the Institute's ground-breaking publication, <u>Outcome Funding</u>, this overview enables practitioners to harness the full power of outcome thinking."

Richard Gutch, Chief Executive
Futerbuilders, London, England

"The Rensselearville Institute's pioneering work in outcomes thinking has helped my organization gain international recognition for achieving powerful results. Now this down to earth, straight talking guide can help you do the same."

Maria Gutierrez
Vice President of Organizational Development
Local Initiatives Support Corporation

"<u>Outcome Frameworks</u> takes us to a new level of understanding on outcomes thinking applications. Its exploration of the history, innovations and variations of outcome practice will be welcome reading for our partners worldwide."

Chuck Holland, Partner and Director
Social Venture Partners Boston

"There is much confusion about "outcomes", but now there is a solution: buy this book. Penna and Phillips have wrapped their arms around a cumbersome, misshapen mountain of material and brought historical and intellectual order to it. Their work signals a field's coming of age and will surely contribute to richer debates about its future."

Lucy Knight
Knight Consulting

'I've experienced the power of an outcome framework in my roles as both public official and non-profit leader. Outcome Frameworks is a welcome addition to the practitioner's toolbox."

Carlton Mitchell, Executive Director
The International Center

"Outcome Frameworks provides a much-needed primer and a solid context for considering and applying outcomes assessment by nonprofit leaders and their funders. The importance of outcomes thinking lies in an organization recognizing the essential need to manage itself to outcomes achievement, using assessment as a regular feedback loop. Penna and Phillips' work is especially important because it helps leaders and managers understand that outcomes thinking is their domain -- not to be relegated to the field of program evaluation, where we've too often fallen prey to 'measuring with a micrometer and making decisions with an ax.'"

Mario Morino, Chairman and Managing Partner
Venture Philanthropy Partners

"An excellent publication! The orientation to language and system-atic comparison of models is a gift to those of us who are trying to figure it out while running as fast as we can. I will use it and will definitely recommend to my colleagues."

Sally T. Prouty, President,
National Association of Service and Conservation Corps

"Outcome Frameworks offers timely and cutting edge perspectives on the major outcome models in use today. As a long-term practitioner, I see the Center for Outcome's leadership as critical for insuring that these powerful ideas are used to enhance results for citizens in need."

Rev. Richard L. Schuster, Executive Director
St. Luke's LifeWorks

"Penna and Phillips' <u>Outcome Frameworks</u> is likely to become an indispensable resource on outcome assessment. It is an all-in-one text that gives readers a useful historical context for evaluation thinking, explains why there is such an emphasis on outcomes in today's private and public sectors, brings together all of the main outcome thinking models, and shows practitioners how to "get to outcomes." The book is at once conceptual and practical, and is surprisingly readable. The authors' and the Institute's experience producing and measuring outcomes comes through. <u>Outcome Frameworks</u> will be important reading for today's practitioners as they think about the outcomes of their work."

Alan M. Schwitzer, Ph.D.
Licensed Psychologist & Associate Professor,
Dept. of Educational Leadership & Counseling
Darden College of Education
Old Dominion University

OUTCOME FRAMEWORKS

An overview for
Practitioners

Robert M. Penna
William J. Phillips

First Edition

The Center for Outcomes
The Rensselaerville Institute   Rensselaerville, New York

About the Rensselaerville Institute

The Rensselaerville Institute, non-profit and independent, is the outcomes place for groups and individuals seeking high achievement. Known as "the think tank with muddy boots," we not only develop new approaches and tools for strong results from programs, but also put them immediately to work with nonprofits, foundations, and government.

About the Center for Outcomes

The Center for Outcomes is the research and development arm of the Institute, with a large emphasis on product development and prototyping. We convene a variety of collaborating organizations in seminars, publications, research, and workshops. Each project, study, or seminar brings together a variety of perspectives and is not restricted by a particular ideology, approach, or toolkit. The focus is on the application of good thinking.

CONTENTS

PREFACE

In 1991, The Rensselaerville Institute published *Outcome Funding: A New Approach to Targeted Grantmaking*. This book introduced a significantly new methodology for assuring that government and philanthropic funds create verifiable gains for individuals, families, and communities. Since its introduction, the Institute's *outcome framework* has been put into practice by several thousand governmental and nonprofit groups throughout North America and several hundred more in the United Kingdom in partnership with The Center for Public Innovation of the UK.

Over the past thirteen years a number of other outcome frameworks have been developed and put into practice. These approaches came about in response to a new reality: times had changed for government and the groups it supports. No longer would stories of intention and activity be enough to satisfy government, philanthropies or individual donors. These donors now demand to know what their resources are accomplishing in terms of changes in the lives and conditions of those being served. Addressing this reality takes more than just rearranging the details of the old success stories; it requires a new approach to how both funders and nonprofit groups think and talk about what they are achieving and, in many cases, in how they act.

This book was written to help practitioners, both those managing nonprofit groups and those financially supporting them, to understand how best to go about selecting and using an outcome approach within the context of this new reality. It does so by addressing these questions:

- What is *Outcome Thinking*, and how is it different from other approaches to funding, planning and management?
- What were its roots and how did it develop?
- What are the primary outcome models currently in use? What are the commonalities? What differentiates them?
- How do nonprofit and government leaders decide what model is the best for their situation?

We should add some clarification about terminology here. Throughout this work, we will use the term *social sector* to refer to the governmental, philanthropic and nonprofit communities. This term, originally coined by Peter F. Drucker in the 1990s to refer to nonprofit organizations specializing in community, social and human services,[1] is used in the spirit of brevity. We acknowledge that we have expanded upon Drucker's original definition, but believe we have kept to the spirit of his meaning. We also recognize that while there are differences among the three sectors we include within the phrase, at their core they are supporting services that enhance the *social* fabric that binds us together. Similarly, we also use the term *outcome thinking* to encompass a wide range of similar outcome related terms. Again this is done to save time and space.

Finally, a word on our choices of outcome models included, and those that we may have missed. We consciously included those that emerged through our research as the most frequently used along with several that presented a new or different perspective or orientation. We apologize for those we might have missed and recognize that strong practice approaches can often elude publication. We hope readers will let us know of other systems or models they find valuable. (Please email us on this or any other reaction at BPhillips@RInstitute.org.) It is our intended outcome that this book serves as a learning tool for a wide range of outcome practitioners and we look forward to hearing from you.

April 2004
Rensselaerville, NY

ACKNOWLEDGEMENTS

The authors would like to express their appreciation to the many people who helped with the development of this book. Among those who provided essential information, valuable insights, key suggestions, supportive guidance and indispensable encouragement were Jed Emerson, Lucy Knight, David Hunter, Paul Brest, Harry Hatry, Peg Hall, Mario Morino, Kay Rockwell, Len Bickman, Mark Freidman, and Alan "Woody" Schwitzer. We would also like to extend our sincere thanks to those including Chris Avery, Bob Giloth, Richard Gutch, Dick Schuster, Chuck Holland, Sally Prouty, Carlton Mitchell, Maria Gutierrez, and Jeanne Mullgrav who took time out of their busy schedules to review and comment upon the manuscript. We want to acknowledge the "cheering section" among the Institute staff, and those including Bryce Johannes and Nancy Hofstadter who worked hard on the book's production. A final and undeniable note of gratitude goes out to our wives, Karen Phillips and Elise Penna, who encouraged us, calmed us, and supported us throughout the work that went into this volume.

The Rensselaerville Institute wishes to express its gratitude to the Achelis and Bodman Foundations and the Annie E. Casey Foundation for their support of the research which made this publication possible.

THE NEW WORLD ORDER

There are probably few leaders or managers of nonprofit enter-prises, governmental agencies, or philanthropic foundations who have not witnessed the growing use of the concept of "*outcomes*" over the past 10 to 15 years. First quietly appearing on the scene more than 20 years ago and initially embraced by a few hearty souls, *outcomes* became a buzzword of the 90s, and a fact of life today for those in the social sector.

What brought about this shift? Why is the "outcome" question being asked *now*, when much more forgiving standards have been applied for so many years? Several forces have been at play:

- The "Reinventing Government" movement stimulated by David Osborne and fast tracked by the passage of the federal Government Performance and Results Act (GPRA) in 1993. With GPRA requirements beginning in 1994, by the year 2000, performance standards - and the outcome focus they required - were a fact of life for most government programs and the groups they support.[2]
- Taxpayer revolts and legislative "looking for results" movements, particularly at the state level, which raised questions about what the public is "buying" with resources expended to address public problems and particularly those designed to ameliorate persistent problem issues.
- The "trickling down" of funding and program responsibility of many former federally led efforts to the state and local levels, in particular those designed to address poverty and health-related issues.

1

- The movement in the health care industry to managed systems that emphasize service and cost controls.

More recently other factors have come into play, including:

- The growing acceptance that government and nonprofit groups can and should be run more like a business, both from a financial management perspective and for mission accomplishment.
- The emergence of new philanthropists, who have challenged conventional perspectives on both the giving and getting of charitable funds.
- The effect the economic downturn has had on the ability of government and the philanthropic community to support the wide range of socially directed programs that have developed over the past 40 years.
- The increased competition for public and charitable funds brought about as a result of the post-9/11/2001 world in which we now live.

Based on these factors, most observers of the nonprofit and government worlds agree that an emphasis on outcomes is here to stay - having gone well beyond the fad status to become an undeniable trend. The fact it has even survived a change in political party affiliation within the federal administration is clear evidence of its permanence on the national scene.

Many leaders of social programs believe that an outcome orientation _should_ be applied to social efforts. "There is an awesome ethical responsibility [for nonprofits] to provide results," one expert has said.[3] Most nonprofits serve the most fragile and disadvantaged populations, he notes, and "There is a _great_ moral burden to be honest and really provide results for these people. It is an ethical issue."[4] As the director of a Midwestern training program added, "We're spending a lot of money...a _lot_ of money. It's only natural that at some point somebody was going to ask what that money was buying. Personally, I think we owe them an answer."

Center stage is no longer dominated by a debate over the question of *whether* an outcome approach is appropriate for the social sector. Instead, the questions occupying most of the attention today are *which* of the various outcome models is the best fit for a given organization, and *how* do leaders and managers go about selecting and implementing an approach that best fits their environment and interests?

We turn our attention to these questions next.

THE SHAPE OF OUTCOME THINKING

What is Outcome Thinking?

While a host of articles and books is available on the market (and on the Internet) with the word *outcome* in the title, covering such disparate disciplines as sports, medicine, and even religion, there are surprisingly few that offer an in-depth examination of the concept of "Outcome Thinking" itself. Additionally, when combined with terms such as *thinking, funding, research, living, evaluation* and *management,*[5] the concept of "*outcomes*" has been used to create a daunting number of hybrid specialties including the use of outcomes as a method for planning, management, and as an evaluation tool.[6]

In defining Outcome Thinking, author and management guru Stephen Covey probably is the most concise with his advice to "begin with the end in mind."[7]   Clawson and Bostrom summarize the relevant research this way:

> *"Highly effective people invest little energy on their existing problem situations. Instead, they focus attention and energy on their desired outcome or on what they want instead of these problems... A key to high performance across all these research contexts has been the ability to develop, articulate and stay focused on a compelling outcome."*[8]

Clawson and Bostrom, demonstrate the power of Outcome Thinking through this simple exercise:

1. Think of a moderately serious problem at work or in your life

2. Pose and answer these questions:
   a. Why do you have the problem?
   b. What caused it?
   c. Who is to blame for it?
   d. What obstacles are there to solving it?
3. Now take the same situation and answer these questions:
   a. What do you want instead of the problem? (Be sure to go beyond merely eliminating the problem.)
   b. What would things be like if the problem was solved? What would we see, hear and feel?
   c. Imagine that the problem is solved; what has been gained?

The difference between focusing on problem-reinforcing questions and outcome-directed ones is palpable, in terms of optimism, energy and hopefulness. This is the essence of outcome thinking. It is much more than mere goal or objective setting. It is a mindset that changes perceptions and the actions that follow. It is a way of envisioning that lifts energy levels and brings new possibilities.

While Clawson and Bostrom stress the critical and important distinction between *outcome-directed* thinking and problem-focused thinking, a more subtle and less acknowledged distinction is between outcome thinking and process or activity thinking. Consider the difference between these two conversations with a nonprofit practitioner portrayed in Table 1.

The first set of questions focuses largely on what goes on inside the organization, while the second centers on what impact these services have outside its doors. While it is certainly helpful to understand what services are offered, that information is only truly useful within the context of what is to be accomplished. Too often, however, the conversations in the social sector are stuck in the process or activity realm.

Table 1: Process-focused versus outcome-focused interview

Process-focused interview:
Q. What does your organization do? A. We provide services to low income residents of our community. Q. What kinds of services? A. We provide group and individual family counseling services. Q. How many people do you serve? A. Last year we provided 500 counseling hours to 125 families.

Outcome-focused interview:
Q. What is your organization hoping to accomplish? A. We are working to improve the parenting skills of abusive families. Q. What kind of skill improvements are you working toward? A. Reductions in use of corporal punishment and increases in uses of positive reinforcers of good behavior, among others. Q. How many families do you help each year? A. Last year we served 500 families and helped 175 to maintain positive changes in their parenting behaviors for at least 6 months. Q. For the coming year, what level of results would make the year a success? A. For the coming year, we are working to improve parenting behavior in 200 families.

Consider how the sets of questions in Table 2 imply different ways of thinking. To further illustrate the point, let's shift the discussion to a context in the social sector with which many readers are familiar. Consider two hypothetical nonprofit groups: Rivervale Community Development Organization (RCDO) and the Hillsdale CDO (HCDO).

Assume for a moment that these groups both serve equally distressed urban communities and both have a staff of 30 and budgets of $5 million. Also assume that all other things are comparable in these two organizations including their missions, the skill level of staff, the care and concern for the community, and the management and leadership skills of the board and executive. But, Rivervale thinks in a process/problem way while Hillsdale is outcome focused. In other words, assume all things between these groups are equal, except for the way they think.

Let's explore the implications of these differences when the executives of these two groups are faced with a series of fairly typical situations, such as these:

- A new board chairperson, who wants to make a difference, is elected from the community.
- A new state funding program for low-income housing is announced.
- A third of the most senior staff has retired over the past six months.
- The community program funding, upon which the organization depends, will be cut significantly in the coming year due to the loss of a major local corporate sponsor.

Let's take the first situation, the appointment of several new board members, and examine how outcome versus process thinking might be applied.

Table 2: Process-oriented versus outcome-oriented questions

Process-Oriented Question	Outcome-Oriented Question
What housing services do you offer?	What community results do you hope to accomplish through your housing services?
What is it that your agency does?	What is your organization striving to achieve?
Describe the service needs your agency meets?	What changes in conditions or behavior are you attempting to effect in the people you serve?
What services must we offer to prevent our community from further deteriorating?	What would be the ideal mix of people and businesses to make our community more desirable?
How can we overcome the learning challenges students bring with them to school?	What skill sets and knowledge must our children possess to be successful?
What public information strategies do you use?	What changes in attitude are you attempting to effect and with what specific groups?

The Rivervale Executive's "process" reaction to this situation might stress the following elements in his briefing to the new board members:

- The high poverty indicators in the community, and the concomitant impact on the residents.
- The negative economic trends developing with a softening economy.
- The magnitude and range of the services the agency offers.
- The staff qualifications, their background and their number of years of service to the agency.
- The financial and personnel challenges facing the agency.

- The difficulty that funding agencies are having finding adequate resources.
- The on-going challenge in finding community leaders to assume board responsibilities.

The Hillsdale Executive Director's reaction, given her Outcome Thinking perspective, would be quite different. She would emphasize these points:

- A summary of last year's accomplishments in helping 20 families attain permanent housing for the first time. While this is only 25% of all families served, given the challenges these families present, the organization is making good progress in this program.

- The organization's on-going commitment to its mission and the vision of creating a highly desirable neighborhood environment for the community's diverse population.

- The current year's targets, and a demonstration of how each of the organization's program outcomes connects to the agency's mission.

- Evidence that, while economic challenges exist, the agency has joined forces with a small but optimistic set of service providers, politicians, and business leaders to lure new businesses to the community and get the attention of state agencies to enhance local resources.

- A recognition that, while program cut-backs are always difficult, a forced reduction in resources might result in a better focus upon what the organization does best, prompting it to drop activities it took on in recent years of generous state budgets.

The differences in perspectives between these two groups are obvious: the difference between a half-full and half-empty viewpoint. While it is certainly true that outcome oriented thinkers must be careful not to lapse into "Cinderella-ism" - a denial of the very real challenges facing the community or organization - there is a growing recognition in the field of organizational development that an increased focus on capabilities and opportunities actually increases their potency.[9]

Author Anne Warfield emphasizes that Outcome Thinking forces individuals to have accountability, to learn the skills they need to reach their desired outcomes in life, whether it's at work, home, or in the community.[10]   A true *outcome* goes beyond what an organization *does*, and rests upon what it accomplishes. An outcome is properly defined in terms of customer focus, what consultant Lucy Knight has called BACKS measures. These are changes in customer **B**ehavior, **A**ttitude, **C**ondition, **K**nowledge, or **S**tatus.[11] In other words, outcomes are not what a program does; rather, they happen *for* those being served *because* of what a program does.

Outcome Thinking is highly powerful when applied in an organizational or personal context:

- It immediately shifts our initial focus from ourselves and what we are doing, to the other person or situation. It forces us to put ourselves in the client's perspective and understand what success will mean from that vantage point.

- It forces us to address at the outset what we are trying to accomplish; or put another way, what defines success.

- It raises the "value-added" question at the start and throughout. Value can only be defined by the meaning and importance placed *by the client or customer* on the product, service or interaction.[12]

The discussion in the preceding pages was intended to give the reader a sense of what Outcome Thinking is, and how it differs from the more traditional, process-oriented thinking and planning with which the social sector has long been familiar. But to truly appreciate the outcome tool, it is necessary to place it into context, to understand where it came from and the forces that influenced its development. We will turn our attentions there next and explore the Lineage of Outcomes.

THE LINEAGE OF OUTCOMES

Few ideas spring forth from a vacuum. Most have an ancestry, a history of concepts and developments that shaped their evolution. Outcome Thinking shares this pattern. To better understand the outcome models and frameworks now being used in the social services environment, an examination of the origins of this thinking is needed. It is worth recognizing, therefore, that, in essence, the outcome movement has two parents - business management and social science evaluation research.

Outcome Thinking's Management Lineage

The earliest forms of management focused on the people who provided the manual labor that comprised the vast majority of work in agrarian, pre-industrial, and even industrial societies. The "management" of work on a farm, a shop or even a factory, was largely the management of the people who were doing that work. Workers were categorized as either lazy or hard working, as strong or weak. The only way known to increase worker output was for workers to work longer, or harder. Frederick Taylor, generally considered to be the father of modern management, was the first to analyze "work" in an attempt to bring about something unprecedented: increased worker productivity.[13] Taylor's insight was that there might be something about the *work* itself that could be improved upon.

Taylor studied industrial workers, analyzing their every action and step. He recorded each motion, the physical effort, and the time it took. Motions not absolutely needed were then eliminated. The remaining actions represented the simplest, fastest and easiest way to obtain the finished product. Within a decade of Taylor's initial efforts, the importance of assessing and improving productivity became widely recognized, and its measurement continues today as a critical tool of increased productivity.[14]

As the post-industrial economy evolved, more and more "work" involved less and less physical labor. The accent of management shifted from a focus on "work" to an accent on "performance."[15] While tasks that required manual labor did continue to receive the attention of management analysts, the main focus shifted from increasing the quantity of the work or effort, to an increase in its "quality." Performance measurement went beyond an assessment of the amount of product a worker generated, to an assessment of how good those products were. This was an important initial step toward Outcome Thinking, because it centered attention, for the first time in a systematic way, upon *results*.

The person most closely associated with this shift is W. Edward Deming, who developed the concept of Total Quality Management, a philosophy of management rooted in an understanding of the power and pervasiveness of variation.[16] All systems, Deming suggested, are subject to a certain amount of deviation in form, condition or appearance, which leads to the eventual erosion of process and product. Understanding variation, therefore, is vital to managing change. For quality to be maintained variation must be reduced. With this new perspective, Deming allowed management to shift its focus from *outputs*, what and how much was being produced, to *outcomes*, the *quality* of what was being produced. An important part of this shift was the focus on measurement, or what has been called Management By Fact. Because of Deming and those who followed and built on his work, it has become an article of organizational faith that "what gets measured gets managed." This focus on measurement, as we

13

shall see in later sections, has had a direct bearing on the development of outcome frameworks in the field of social sector services.

After Taylor and Deming, the management genealogy of Outcome Thinking leads to Donald Kirkpatrick's four-level assessment guide for corporate training programs.[17] Kirkpatrick suggested that all training programs should be assessed from four basic perspectives, as shown if Figure 1.

Level 1: Participant reaction to the program - Participants' reactions have important consequences for learning, because, although a positive reaction does not guarantee learning, a negative reaction almost certainly reduces its possibility. In other words, if they don't *like* it, they won't learn from it.

Level 2: Participant learning - To what extent did those engaged advance in the familiar measures of skill, knowledge, or attitude?

Level 3: Impact on participant behavior - To what degree were the newly acquired skills, knowledge, or attitudes applied in the everyday environment of the learner?

Level 4: Effect on business results - At this level, the impact of the training on the financial or other business results of the organization is determined.

Figure 1: In Kirkpatrick's four-level model, each successive evaluation level is built on information provided by the lower level.[18]

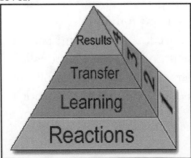

Kirkpatrick's system has become the standard for business-based training programs, and it has directly influenced the evolution of Outcome Thinking, particularly in the public sector, where it has lent valuable insights into the *learning* and resultant behavior change upon which so many programs are based.

But if this early management theory was the only source of Outcome Thinking as we know it today, it would probably be indistinguishable from Six Sigma, TQM, Reengineering, and a host of other theories that have been applied to the corporate world in the last few decades. However, we know that *corporate* management theory is different because of the one central variable that it centers around: **profit**. The corporate bottom line, the need to make a profit, and the need to position an organization to be able to continue those profits in the future, are the considerations that form the main dividing line between the corporate world and the governmental and nonprofit sectors. Governmental and nonprofit organizations exist not to make a profit, but to *serve*. This requires a different calculus, a different measure of outcomes. It also explains the other source of Outcome Thinking as we know it today, the other part of its "family tree." That source is the discipline of evaluation.

The Contribution of Evaluation

Former New York City Mayor Ed Koch used to revel in the opportunity to return the greetings of passers-by with the question, "How'm I doin'?" For the Mayor, that question, tossed back to people who would greet him, wave, or call to him on the street, was a quick test of his effectiveness and his popularity. But even though Mr. Koch turned it into a light-hearted trademark, the query is basic to all government-supported institutions.

While the answer to this question for politicians and their policies is provided periodically at the ballot box, much more subtle and targeted approaches are needed to assess the effectiveness of the

15

many programs that the general population comes in contact with on a daily basis. The development of those approaches took place within the field of social science-based evaluation, a field with the explicit mission to improve the quality of social programs.[19]

As early as 1874, growing concerns with public health led to the first concerted efforts at collecting programmatic information regarding the effectiveness of public policies in the U.S., and by 1907 the New York City Bureau of Municipal Research was collecting data on social conditions. These early studies were more descriptive than evaluative, however, and it was not until much later did the need for "reliable and valid" measures become widely recognized.

In 1969, the Urban Institute completed an extensive assessment of the "evaluations" of federally sponsored programs and concluded that such evaluation was "almost non-existent."[20] Too many programs, the study concluded, were being based upon untested or even unsound assumptions, on tradition or on "common sense." The suggested solution was a 4-step process:[21]

1. Separating out the underlying assumptions of programs and initiatives;
2. Questioning those assumptions;
3. Subdividing objectives into intermediate steps;
4. Introducing criterion of *performance* instead of effort.

While the idea of *impacts* beyond a program's *outputs* and *outcomes* was still some years away, this study and others that followed sowed the seeds of this train of thought.

One of the most influential figures in the development of evaluation theory was Donald T. Campbell, called by some, "perhaps the greatest" methodologist of modern times.[22] Campbell is credited with setting the basic intellectual direction for evaluation as it is used today. It was Campbell who was responsible for reminding the developing field of evaluation that its overarching goal is to eliminate rival and competing hypotheses through the simplest means possible. He is best known within evaluation circles for coining the concept of quasi-experimental design and for advocating use of experimental methods for evaluation.[23]

The quasi-experimental research designs Campbell presented were meant to standardize social experimentation, and particularly evaluation of social policies. Campbell's ideal was an experimenting society, in which all policies would be viewed as hypotheses and tested in a standardized way before implementation.

Campbell also believed there was nothing particularly wrong with the failure of a program. Failure should be a source of learning and should not be explained away or excused. Instead, he suggested, it is a great motivator of change and innovation. Campbell preached that only when people feel sufficiently secure with the knowledge that failure is not an end, but a new beginning, will practitioners embrace evaluation as a tool rather than a seeing it as a problem to be avoided or overcome.[24] It was Campbell's influence that is largely responsible for evaluation's increasingly evidence-based format - a direct precursor to the outcome-based frameworks we will explore later.

Another important "uncle" in the evolution of the outcome movement was Claude Bennett. Writing in 1975, Bennett stressed that "evaluation is not an end in itself [and] is only worth doing if it helps in making decisions about program continuation, priorities and modifications."[25] He introduced the notion of using this emerging discipline as a *management tool*. A year earlier, Pamela Horst and her colleagues had noted that one of the major stumbling blocks to effective and *useful* evaluation was that most evaluations were not designed to support decision-making, were not geared toward decision-makers, nor were their findings adequately communicated to these decision-makers.[26] *Why then*, Bennett asked, *were these evaluations being done?* His implication was that evaluation divorced from management was little more than judgment, and of little value to programs, implementers or funders. Also implicit was the notion of *a learning process*.

Prior to Bennett the emphasis of evaluation had been on *accountability*, upon the need to demonstrate to funders and to the public that programs *worked*. This became especially true in the face of the intractability of many of the problems these programs were designed to address: if poverty, crime, substance abuse and a host of other ills remained, in spite of billions of dollars expended upon their eradication, of what *use* were these programs? This question was at the heart of the "nationwide accountability movement."[27] Bennett, while recognizing the importance of this perspective, cautioned that merely evaluating programs to see if they "worked" was not enough. Rather, the data should also be utilized for "modification," to acknowledge what mistakes were made and to *learn* from them.

Bennett became best known for his 7-step, *chain of events* hierarchy. Beginning with *inputs*, he connected a series of steps that led eventually to the accomplishment of goals. Put another way, Bennett introduced the concept of a sequential logic to social programs.

Joseph Wholey and a team of Urban Institute researchers added several crucial pieces of the puzzle in the mid-70s when they, like Bennett, asked penetrating questions about the evaluations that were going on at the time, questions like "Why were those in charge of programs, and those who were evaluating them unable to join their efforts in a way that lent to significant improvement in program performance?" Wholey's team sought ways to make evaluations more likely to be useful by *helping program managers*.[28]

Horst describes a significant breakout of two distinct dynamics involved in the use of evaluations:

- The interface between evaluators and users of evaluations
- The interface between evaluators and the programs being evaluated.

This work was significant in that it differentiated among the audiences of evaluation, and among their respective needs. Wholey recognized that program managers did not need or benefit from the type of information that evaluations typically provided to funders and policy-makers. He concluded that the necessary kind of management information was not the focus of most conventional evaluations. Developing a concept called "Program Evaluability," Wholey argued that many programs were not designed to be meaningfully evaluated, primarily due to three reasons:

1. The lack of clear definitions. In other words, the target problem, program interventions, expected outcomes and desired impacts were often not sufficiently defined as to be measurable.
2. The absence of a consistent logic. Many programs lacked a clear linkage between resource expenditures, the intervention itself and the predicted program impacts.
3. A dearth of management skills. Too many program leaders had little training, experience or authority to act on evaluation findings.[29]

While Bennett stressed the need for an inherent logic linking the steps or stages of an evaluation hierarchy, Wholey and Horst went further to suggest that this logic should be determined and applied *before* the evaluation stage. If we are to *evaluate* to any degree of success and validity, they were saying, we must *plan* along lines that make evaluation possible and meaningful.

The evolution toward modern Outcome Thinking was almost complete. Len Bickman added another very significant contribution when he focused the attention of thinkers and practitioners on the need for program theory. "All too commonly," he wrote, "programs seem to grow from notions and ideas," rather than from a sound, testable theory. Bickman urged the adoption of program theory that would be "the construction of a plausible and sensible model of how a program is supposed to work."[30]   According to Bickman, sound theories would contain these elements:

• Clarity on the set of cause-and-effect relationships within a given situation, along with the rationale for a specific programmatic intervention;

• Scientific explanations, implicit theories, models of inputs, processes and outputs, and policy statements; and

• The resources, activities and outcomes of programs, and the causal assumptions connecting them.

Bickman was making a powerful argument for the application of outcome focused thinking *before* a program or intervention was implemented...and way before the evaluation stage. For a discipline that had grown as a means toward better, more useful evaluations, this was a revolutionary call for the use of outcome frameworks as a planning and management tool.

We clearly recognize that others, including Carol Weiss, Marvin Atkin, and Michael Quinn Patton, have made important contributions to the evolution of evaluation, and, in turn, to Outcome Thinking; those contributions, however, are not within the scope of this work.   Rather, it has been our intention to provide the social sector practitioner with an overview of the roots that have contributed to the development of the outcome frameworks and approaches in use today.

What we have seen is that the concept did not have one clear line of development, or one clear origin. Early thinkers in corporate management opened the door by asking questions regarding results and performance. Twenty years into the last century, observers of social programs began to shed light on the need for a clear definition of objectives if questions regarding those programs and their effect were to be answered. As more experience was gained, the need for sound, testable logic linking assumptions to actions was recognized. The concept of applying tests to this logic before program implementation was a major leap. Other refinements were added and changed the emerging notion of outcome thinking from an abstract concept accessible only to a few, into a tool that could be utilized and applied by decision-makers and program directors across a wide array of programs and purposes.

But where is the discipline today? How is it defined? What are the various outcome models and what makes one different from the next? How does an organization decide which model is best for its needs? These questions are the focus of the sections that follow.

THE LANGUAGE OF OUTCOMES

To engage in outcome thinking or, for that matter, any thinking, language is essential. We conceptualize within a framework of language; we use language to communicate with ourselves and others.

The language of outcomes, therefore, is at the core of its power and potential to change and inspire. The paradox is this: any organization that chooses the outcome path must eventually come to grips with the choice of an outcome language for use within the organization and within its culture. However, once this choice is made, communication with those outside that culture will be more difficult, at least initially. Nonetheless, a clear terminology for a limited number of key concepts, and the discipline to use these terms precisely, is ultimately a terrific boost toward improved communication with both those who operate within and outside an organization's "system."

What makes this particularly challenging in the social sector is the multiplicity of professions that populate its many programs. Take for example the field of social services. Any moderately-sized organization probably employs staff from the disciplines of social work, psychology, medicine, education, business manage-ment, accounting, and public administration, among others, each bringing with them their own language and values gained through professional training and reinforced in their work. Add to this the specialized language that is present in each social services specialty, i.e. child welfare, homelessness, juvenile services, etc., and it is not surprising that communication is the most often cited challenge to high performance. Little wonder that helping groups take on the language of outcomes is challenging and sometimes resisted.

But since this language *is* so important, before we review the major models and frameworks currently in use in the social sector, let's review a few concepts and definitions common to most of them:

Input: The resources that go into a program or service, including staff time, facilities, equipment, and management overhead. Inputs also may refer to service activities like counseling, materials, training programs, etc. Essentially inputs are all the things that define the organization and what it offers. Inputs answer the question *"What goes into the services you provide?"*

Output: The end-point good or service that is produced by a given process or activity. Outputs are generally not individual client specific, but are described in overall volume terms. While outputs have clear outcome implications, they are not the same as outcomes.
Outputs answer the question: *"What tangible evidence is there that your service or program was delivered?"*
Table 3 provides some examples.

Outcome: For obvious reasons, this term is clearly the most important one used in an outcome framework, and it is the term that has the most different uses. In some cases it is used to describe *projected* positive changes in condition, behavior, attitude or status of an individual or group served by a program. In other models it is used to describe what has already been accomplished. In still other cases, outcomes reflect the core purpose or mission of a program or organization, its vision for success in the future.

Table 3: Output examples

Service Type	Typical Output
Training	Number of people trained Curriculum produced
Strategic Planning	The written plan
Counseling	Persons served over a period (day, month or year)
Housing program	Number of new units built or rehabilitated
Substance abuse treatment	Number of treatment completions

Outcomes are the bottom-line results for a program or organization. To be most relevant, outcomes must be considered achievable by a particular program or service. Or put another way, they need to be within the program's realm of control or influence.

Outcomes typically answer the following essential questions:

- What will be different for those served once they have received the program's *outputs*?
- What is your program's or agency's ultimate vision for success?

Table 4 displays sample outcomes for a range of social sector programs, along with typical outputs for these programs.

But outputs and outcomes are not the only by-products of a program or system. There are several

Table 4: Outcomes examples

Program	Output	Outcomes
Affordable Housing	Housing units created or rehabbed	Persons living in improved housing and staying current on rent payments
Employment	Job training	Placement in a job; job retention for a specific period of time; the gaining of fringe benefits such as medical insurance by those employed or hired
Community Loan Programs	Loans made	Persons using loan funds to increase self-suffi-ciency; paying back the loans

other terms with which the reader should become familiar. This list is not meant to be all-inclusive, but rather to introduce the reader to the most central concepts common to most outcome frameworks. Practitioners will certainly come into contact with terms not on this list, as well as alternative definitions or uses for the terms outlined.

Impact: This term generally refers to the broader or cumulative effect that accrues from the achievement of *outcomes for individuals*. For example, the cumulative *impact* of achieving the *outcome* of helping low income residents attain improved housing might include the removal of visual blight throughout the neighborhood, reduction of crime

in the neighborhood, improved performance in
school by residents' children, increased business
activity or higher property values in a neighborhood.

Performance Target:

A projected level of *outcome* performance established at the onset of a program or service period.
Targets typically define success for a period of time
and for a set of persons to be served. The use of
targeting is a critical element for the effective use of
outcome thinking in an organizational context.
Targets may be presented with time frame considerations - generally long and short term. A sample
target would be that 25 of the 50 families receiving
counseling will reduce the inappropriate use of
corporal punishment from five times per week to
no more than twice per week and will maintain
that improvement for at least six months.

To help the reader understand how these concepts are applied in a
social sector environment, let's consider a community-based
employment and training program. The *inputs* are the people who
enroll in the program, the expertise the program's staff brings to
the situation and the program services offered, which in this case
is a six week training program on how to develop a resume, get a
job and handle a job interview. Other inputs include the number
of training sessions and staff hours offered to the trainees and
other things like the facilities and materials.

Outputs would be the number of young people completing the
training and receiving a certificate. In this example the number
completing the program in a given year is 100. This does not
meet the test of an *outcome*, because in most cases the purpose of a
training program like this is not *just* to produce credentialed

graduates. This program is designed and funded to help get folks *placed* in jobs, and often to get them to *retain* those jobs for at least a minimum period. This is the *outcome* description for this type of program.

Now let's assume that in this instance the *performance target* is to enable 75 of the 100 people completing the program to get a job. But we have to ask, is that enough? In this example, if the target was left as stated, "*to enable 75 out of 100 program graduates to get a job,*" this could be met if they all worked one day at McDonald's and were then all fired or quit. If we added the requirement that they should keep that job without specifying for how long, employment of only a week or two might allow the program to claim success. If however, the target was defined as "*75 out of 100 trainees will get a 35 hour per week job, at a wage of at least $8 an hour, and keep that job for at least six months,*" the program's potential service implications would be significantly different.

Let's return to our hypothetical housing and community development agencies noted earlier, Rivervale/Hillsdale, and describe how the terms noted above might be applied to this type of publicly supported organization.

Inputs: A staff of housing developers and community organizers providing housing renovation along with tenant support and money management services.

Output: The creation of units of new and rehabilitated housing and the delivery of housing support services to tenants.

Outcome: (vision for success) Low income families reside in improved housing and remain there for at least 12 months while maintaining the properties at acceptable community standards.

Impact: Community values will increase as a result of the cumulative effect of improved housing stock and families meeting increased maintenance and cleanliness standards.

27

Targets: • 30 families move into newly renovated apartments
during the year, an increase from 15 last year; and
• 10 of the 15 families placed in the prior year retain
their housing for 12 months without threat of eviction
for either failure to pay rent or for violating housing
maintenance or management requirements.

In this example the *targets*, particularly the second one, requires
the agency to go beyond housing renovation services to include
services to tenants that will increase the likelihood that they will
retain their housing for the 12 month period under the conditions
described, i.e. that they pay their rent on time and maintain the
property to defined standards. We are confident that the reader
understands the significant implication for the changes implied by
these kinds of targets or outcomes for service providers and those
funding these programs.

In looking for an example that would help illustrate the power
and logic of an outcome framework and the thinking behind it,
we found the work of Dr. Alan M. Schwitzer to be helpful.
Schwitzer, an Associate Professor at the Department of
Educational Leadership & Counseling at the Darden College of
Education of Old Dominion University, developed The Chain of
Effects Framework[31] as a method of assessing student service
outcomes within campus settings. Working from Michael Quinn
Patton's "utilization-focused" approach to evaluation research,[32]
Schwitzer devised a three-step method of planning for and assessing outcomes. It assumes that effective programs must be based
on an explicit theory of action, which is logically linked to a
"chain of objectives" that, if followed, will lead to success. This
chain is based on three levels of related goals.

• Immediate-level outcome goals that focus on program
implementation and the initial experiences of students who
participate

- Intermediate goals that capture specific changes in student behavior, attitude, condition or status that come about from their engagement in the program
- Ultimate goals that refer to long-term positive changes or impacts in students

These goals are tied together to create a set of causal links in a hierarchical chain of objectives. According to this hierarchy, accomplishing *implementation goals* is necessary to achieve *inter-mediate-level goals*. These, in turn, are required to accomplish the *ultimate-level outcomes*. This, then, is the "chain of effects."

Let's apply this approach to the Rivervale/Hillsdale housing program example used earlier. Remember the outcome (vision for success) for the program is this:

Low-income families reside in improved housing and remain there for at least 12 months while maintaining their housing properties to acceptable community standards.

- First, the program has to attract clients who meet the program's requirements and understand what the program is designed to accomplish. This may not be as simple as it sounds, given that what many low-income families want is to address their immediate problem of inadequate living quarters. But if the program fails to help clients buy in to the program's intended outcomes, the chances of success are greatly reduced. So, finding appropriate clients and getting them to buy into the program's goals and projected outcomes represent Schwitzer's immediate-level outcome goals.
- Next, program staff must begin moving clients on the road toward the ultimate outcome of "retaining and maintaining" improved housing. This might involve helping them through the housing application process, getting them to enroll in and complete training sessions on basic budgeting

and home maintenance skills. The program staff also needs
to understand the clients' housing needs based on family
membership, location to jobs or other services.
Accomplishing these tasks, what Schwitzer calls *intermediary goals*, is clearly critical to achieving success in terms of
the stated *outcome*. We should add here that another significant accomplishment might include the rehabilitation or
even construction of the new housing unit itself. Clearly it
is a major step in this particular Chain of Effects, and one
that often absorbs the attention and resources of most
housing programs. But as can be seen, while rehabilitating
the housing unit is a critical rung on the ladder of success, it
in itself does not equate to achieving the *outcome*.
Accomplishing this step and helping move the client family
in would be, in Schwitzer's framework, a key intermediate
goal or possibly even a longer-term positive change. But it
still does not yet achieve the *outcome*.

- Once housing placement occurs, considerable work remains
  for the staff. Achieving the 12-month "retaining and
  maintaining" target, could involve as much or more work
  than was required to accomplish the earlier goals. Helping
  clients use the budgeting skills they were taught and helping
  them deal with unexpected emergencies and changes in
  their situations, often present major barriers to the accomplishment of such "long-term positive changes."

- "Longer-term impacts" in this situation, would include
  examining improvements in neighborhood conditions and
  possibly even the accumulated positive effects on the
  family's life, including children's school performance and
  other indicators of family stability.

As a practitioner himself, Schwitzer demonstrated that the effective use of Outcome Thinking goes beyond envisioning and
focusing on the outcome. It requires in most cases the consideration of a *system* of interrelated parts, steps and expectations. Later

goals cannot be achieved unless preliminary ones are accomplished; ultimate success depends upon initial successes. Similarly, his work tells us that effective Outcome Thinking does not merely assume linkages between steps in a progression; instead, it accounts for and demonstrates them. It asks — and answers — those smaller questions, like what sequence of skills are needed to help low-income families be prepared for the challenges they will inevitably face after they receive their new home? These questions exist in the gaps between the bigger questions that usually get the most attention — like how do we go about rehabilitating poor quality housing within budget and schedule? In the outcome models discussions that follow, the reader will see the vital importance in the effective use of Outcome Thinking when considering these intermediary issues.

There are a variety of ways to consider this issue of outcomes and the language used to describe them. In addition to those already described, we offer two other approaches that may prove useful. The first is the distinction between *instrumental* and *ultimate* outcomes. First used by Rosen and Proctor in 1981,[33] this approach defines *ultimate* outcomes as the goals for which the program is undertaken in the first place — the reduction of poverty, or insuring that all children are successful learners, would be two common examples. Placing and maintaining unemployed individuals in long term jobs at above minimum wage and with benefits would be an associated *instrumental* outcome. Increasing the number of fourth grade children who read at grade level would be another *instrumental* outcome.

This framework again demonstrates the importance of establishing intervening stages of progress — whether they are called "stages," "steps," or "milestones" — as outcome goals in their own right. They should be separable targets that a program can track and which are directly associated with the accomplishment of the "ultimate goals."

Another way of looking at this would be to consider outcomes along a continuum of *primary, secondary* and *tertiary*, which roughly align with Schwitzer's different goal levels, as explained in Figure 2.

To use a housing redevelopment agency as an example, the *inputs* are the funds that support the effort, the volunteers who may help with the rehabilitation and the expertise the program's staff brings to the situation. The *output* could be described in terms of the number of housing units successfully restored and made available to local residents. But this output, the refurbished units, represents an incomplete result. A family occupying each of those units is the target we are really seeking. We call this occupancy rate, the program's principal effects, its *primary, direct, immediate* or *instrumental* outcome. Remember, outcomes are not what a program *does*; rather, outcomes happen *because* of what a program does.

Figure 2: Primary, secondary, tertiary outcomes versus Schwitzer's
           different goal levels

Primary	Direct Outcomes	Immediate Outcomes	Instrumental Outcomes
		↓	↓
Secondary	Indirect Outcomes	Intermediary Outcomes	
		↓	↓
Tertiary	Impacts	Long-term Outcomes	Ultimate Outcomes

Yet even here, we need a sense of the longer-term effects of programs and systems. Many things can produce immediate, tangible results. But we also know from experience that most things in life also have secondary, or ripple effects. These "secondary effects," these things that happen after and as a result of a system's *outcomes*, can be seen as its *secondary* or *intermediary* outcomes, or its impacts. The strengthened families experiencing more stability as a result of living in the refurbished housing units would be an example. Finally, there are the longer term effects to be considered or assessed. Depending upon the mission behind the program, these could be seen as the *ultimate, tertiary, indirect* or *long-term* outcomes. Illustrations of this, if we stick to our housing example, would be the neighborhood stability created by the presence of those families on a given street, or even the economic impact those families have on the local corner grocery store. These are long-term outcomes.

* * * * *

This section was designed to help the reader understand the language of Outcome Thinking. We also began to explore the perspectives and approaches that are at the core of the outcome movement. We will next examine some of the outcome models and frameworks in use in the social sector and continue the discussion of the practical considerations they imply.

THE MAJOR SOCIAL SECTOR OUTCOME MODELS

It should come as no surprise that as the concept of outcomes and outcome-based decision-making has spread and grown in popularity, a number of different approaches have been developed for applying this thinking. These approaches are generally called "outcome models," and many in the social sector have at least heard of some of these models, even if they are not completely familiar with them. In this section, we are going to survey some of the leading models, noting their differences and similarities.

The Project Logic Model

The Logic Model is probably the most widely applied outcome model today. It is used by thousands of organizations, in the U.S., Canada and beyond. Recommended by The United Way of America and the Kellogg Foundation, among other funding groups, it is a diagrammatic representation that provides a road map for a given program, showing what it is supposed to do, with whom, and why.[34]

The model generally includes these concepts and terms:

- Target group(s): the individuals, groups or communities to receive the program
- Resources to be brought to bear on the targeted problem: personnel, volunteers, physical resources, financial resources, information on target group needs, etc.
- Activities: action steps required to achieve program outcomes
- Components: groups of conceptually related activities, such as educating, social marketing, etc.

- Outcomes or objectives: changes or benefits resulting from activities, process, intermediate and long term

Some logic models also include *indicators*, the purpose of which is to assess whether program goals have been achieved. Figure 3 show an example of a typical project logic diagram.

Figure 3: Example of a typical project logic diagram[35]

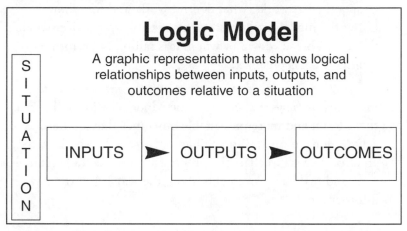

In 1998, with the publication of its Evaluation Handbook, the Kellogg Foundation added its endorsement of the model, citing multiple benefits from its use, including:

> *Program design benefits*: According to the Kellogg Foundations, use of the Logic Model allows staff to stay better focused on outcomes, connect interim outcomes to long-term outcomes, link activities and processes to desired outcomes, and keep underlying program assumptions at the forefront of their minds. The process of creating a program logic model, the Foundation states, clarifies thinking about the program, how it was originally intended to work, and what adaptations may need to be made once the program is operational.

A base from which to conduct ongoing evaluation of the program: The Kellogg Foundation maintains that the Logic Model spells out how a program is intended to produce desired outcomes, thereby helping implementers decide more systematically which pieces of the program to study in determining whether or not initial assumptions were correct. The Logic Model, the Foundation suggests, helps focus the evaluation on measuring each set of events in the model to see what happens, what works, what doesn't work, and for whom. Using the model, evaluation teams are able to discover where the model breaks down or where it is failing to perform as originally conceptualized.

An effective approach for evaluating complex initiatives with intangible or long-term outcomes: the Model is said to illustrate the interim and more measurable outcomes that are needed to achieve long-term and intangible outcomes, thereby providing an effective way to chart the progress of more complex initiatives and make improvements along the way based on new information.

Within the Logic Model format, directional arrows demonstrate the causal relationships between elements of the model; it is also within these arrows that the "logic" of the model is contained.

There are three versions of the Logic Model generally used. The first is the *Outcome Model*, which displays the interrelationships of long-term goals and shorter-term objectives. Sometimes called a step model or milestone model, this version is useful in illustrating longer-term, intangible, or hard-to-measure outcomes.

A second version is called the *Activities Model*. This is a process-focused illustration, often depicting the linkages between various actions, which combine to describe a program or initiative. Particularly appropriate for indicating antecedent-consequent relationships, where programmatic gains are sequential in nature and the success of later ones depends upon the successful attainment of earlier ones, the *Activities Model* works well for complex initiatives that involve many layers of activities and/or multiple partners.

The third type of logic model is the *Theory Model*. This model links theoretical constructs to explain the underlying assumptions of a program. The intention is to describe why the program is expected to work as it does. While a suggested use of this version is the illustration of especially complex, multi-faceted initiatives,[36] the resulting diagrams can often be extremely confusing, their "logic" often lost in a knot of convoluted causal arrows.

Proponents of the logic model point to its utility in the program planning process, particularly as a way to promote greater stakeholder involvement, greater acceptance and commitment to the program, and increased commitment to the use of evaluation results. They suggest that the model development process can lead to a shared vision of the program through discovery and negotiation.[37] Logic models are often best used to depict major, recurring items in an organization or program.[38]

There can be no denying that the Logic Model can be a useful tool, particularly at the earliest stages of a project. It allows funders, stakeholders and staff to grasp at a glance the goals of a program. As a top-level depiction of the flow of materials and processes needed to produce the results desired by the organization or program,[39] it clearly delineates the broad chain of events required for the program's success. It allows for relatively easy modification, as additional actors are discovered or engaged in the program.

For describing a program in the broadest strokes, there is probably no better tool. However, the model has several limitations. One is that is presents issues and processes in a linear fashion, even

Figure 4: Example of casual linkages in Logic Model[40]

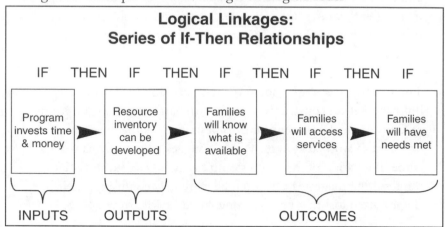

though many are decidedly non-linear. The circuitous routes that progress often takes in real life are not well represented within the Logic Model.

Causal linkages, represented by the arrows within the model, are a key component of the Logic Model, forming a series of "If/Then" statements, but they also include the model's assumptions. By way of example, let's consider Figure 4.

In this statement, "*if* families know what resources are available, *then* families will access services and have needs met." A central assumption here is that families _will_ access these services. Thus, various factors, even lethargy, which might prevent or dissuade families from doing so, are not accounted for. The Logic Model thus focuses upon *expected* outcomes. Outcomes that are coincidental or the products of multiple factors are not dealt with well within this model. Finally, the Logic model does not address the question of whether a program is doing the right thing.[41]

This is not to say that more complicated or even nonlinear systems cannot be represented within the Logic Model. However, attempts to do so often result in schematics that border upon those criticized as "indecipherable" by Micklethwait;[42] their "logic" becomes increasingly difficult to comprehend, no less to follow, as more variables, steps and If/Then statements are included. See Figure 5 for one such example here.

The Logic Model is good at helping organizations set targets and even broad strategies. Yet it can often leave the *tactics* largely unaddressed. This is largely by design, the recommended level of detail in a Logic Model being that "sufficient for the reader to grasp the major items that go into an organization or program, what occurs to those inputs, the various outputs that results and the overall benefits, impacts (or outcomes) that occur, and to which groups of people.[43] This design decision is a major limitation of use of the model: it is very difficult to use as a management tool by nonprofit agencies and those who fund them. There is no element of the approach that enables groups to monitor their own interim performance. Using the *First Things First* chart below, how will the organization know, for example, if it is being successful in "increasing student engagement (C1)"? Neither the chart nor the model shed light upon how many students must be engaged so as to ensure that "student performance is enhanced (B)." At the root of this problem is the fact that "student engagement" itself is not clearly defined in behavioral terms. Does this mean they show up most or every day, or that they are completing all or some assignments on time and correctly?

The Logic Model, like most other outcome approaches, rests heavily upon assumptions. It lays out what the program is *expected* to achieve and how it is *expected* to work, based on an *expected* chain of events.[44] In the *First Things First* model, it is assumed that student engagement will increase, but nowhere in the model is it specified _how_ these changes will take place. As the United Way of Milwaukee states, the "Program Logic Model is a visual

Figure 5: First Things First School-Site Reform Theory Change[45]

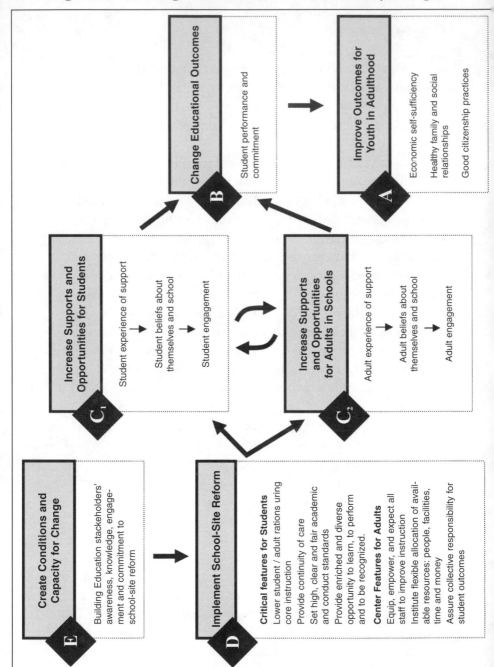

depiction of *how a program theoretically works* to foster change..."
(emphasis added).[46] This accent on the *theoretical* is a key limitation of the model.

Put another way, the Logic Model is a simple picture, based upon
a chain of connections showing what a program is supposed to
accomplish.[47] As such, it illustrates the theory behind a program
to a far greater extent than it does the actions that will be required
to accomplish the program's goals.

By way of example, the Western Regional Center for the
Application of Prevention Technologies advises that, "In order to
build a useful logic model, [programs] will need to answer the
following questions:

- What are the risk and protective factors to be addressed?
  (the goals)
- What services and activities will be provided?
  (the strategies)
- Who will participate in or be influenced by the program?
  (the target group)
- How will these activities lead to expected outcomes?
  (the Theory of Change or "If-Then" Statement)
- What immediate changes are expected for individuals,
  organizations, or communities? (the short-term outcomes)
- What changes would the program ultimately like to create?
  (the long-term impacts)."[48]

The "logic" of the model is expressed in the reliance upon the
program's "Theory of Change," upon a series of "If/Then" statements, and upon "expected" changes and outcomes. As Mr. Spock
might observe, however, the model is only as sound as the logic.
This too is a central limitation of the system.

These cautions noted, however, the Logic Model *has* unquestionably been found to be useful as an evaluation tool. By allowing programs to focus upon certain previously identified goals, it eases measurement of the degree to which those goals were attained. Using a Logic Model-based evaluation, agencies that might have had difficulty in the past citing actual gains made by clients, are now able to state that:

- "More than 87% of 254 clients' goals toward improvement in targeted areas were met;"
- "85% of 274 participating youths showed gains of at least one year in reading and math skills;"
- "More than half of 8,540 participating Scouts were involved in community service activities, completing 955 projects."[49]

Who, then, should use the Logic Model? Certainly those organizations whose funders prescribe its use should employ it. Most organizations in the earliest phases of Outcome Thinking would also find it fairly simple to master, and it *is* a good introduction to concepts that underlay most outcome frameworks. Organizations that require a way for demonstrating complex processes in a simpler, easy-to-grasp manner, may also find the model useful. By way of illustration, the Louisiana Challenge, a program of the Louisiana State Department of Education, uses the logic model to demonstrate the process by which it hopes to raise the technological readiness of students in the state's schools.

Clearly, such processes as curriculum development, school readiness and school-to-work transition are quite complicated. The Logic Model is not intended to downplay that complexity. However, the beauty of the model in this instance is that it allows the "Big Picture," so to speak, to be captured and conveyed, without being bogged down in the details of the constituent processes. For this task, and for many specific others, the Logic Model is particularly well suited, and certainly ought to be recommended.

The Balanced Scorecard

If the Logic Model favors one side of Outcome Thinking's family tree, bearing an unmistakable resemblance to the evaluation work from which it derived, the Balanced Scorecard (BSC) just as strikingly bears all the hallmarks of corporate management theory, the other side of the gene pool behind outcomes. For while the BSC is increasingly being utilized as a results-oriented framework by public and nonprofit organizations,[50] it was originally and specifically designed as an outcome model to address the emerging needs of corporate entities.

Created by Robert S. Kaplan and David P. Norton, the BSC traces its roots to a study undertaken by the Norton Institute in the mid-1990s. The study was motivated by a belief that existing performance measures, relying as they did primarily upon financial accounting, were becoming obsolete. In an increasingly complex operating environment, Kaplan and Norton concluded, these traditional measures were in fact *hindering* business organizations' ability to create future economic value.[51] The problem lay in the fact that even though there were a variety of measures available to corporate managers, ROI, ROCE, P/R, and others among them, they all essentially focused upon dollars. They were, in other words, a variety of ways to look at the same variable. Worse still, they were all measures of *past* performance, and gave little guidance for future action or growth.

Kaplan and Norton's insight was that a multiplicity of variables needed to be managed and accounted for. Moreover, it was not enough for these variables to merely be placed side-by-side, the approach taken in the French outcome system, the *Tableau de Bord*.[52] The *Tableau* is based upon the metaphor of a dashboard, its various "gauges" depicting a number of simultaneous indicators. This approach leaves the inter-relatedness of these variables largely to others to explain. What was needed, Kaplan and

Norton insisted, was not a cockpit dashboard, but a model more along the lines of a flight simulator, something that handled multiple measures, reflecting multiple coincident processes, and linked them into a consistent and mutually reinforcing whole.[53] The target of their effort was nothing less than the development of a completely new performance model. The BSC authors also foresaw that "the best use" of their new tool would be not merely as a measurement system to track performance, but to "manage strategy,"[54] to communicate within and to align organizations to new, longer-term goals and strategies. Thus was conceived the multidimensional BSC, a tool that allows managers to simultaneously look at the performance of an organization from four separate-but-related perspectives.

- Customer Perspective: *How do customers see us?*
- Internal Capabilities Perspective: *At what must we excel?*
- Innovation and Learning Perspective: *Can we continue to improve and create value?*
- Financial Perspective: *How do our owners/shareholders see us?*[55]

The "balance" that the model offers is between short- and long-term objectives, between financial and non-financial measures, between lagging and leading indicators, between performance measures and performance drivers, and, finally, between internal and external indices of success.

The Scorecard begins with the premise that strategy is a set of hypotheses about cause and effect. While this is true of *any* outcome model, the properly designed plan should identify and make explicit the sequence of hypotheses about the cause-and-effect relationships between outcome measures and the performance drivers of those outcomes.[56]

Inherently designed to both measure *and* impact an organization's long-term prospects, the Scorecard emphasizes an organization's intent by highlighting strategic goals and linking them to performance measures. It broadens the focus of management from relatively short-term goals to include issues that affect sustainable long-term performance, and focuses management's attention on those capabilities - the performance drivers - that will be critical to realizing the strategic intent. This emphasis on performance drivers is one of the characteristics that sets BSC apart from other outcome frameworks, for the *Scorecard* not only asks where do we want to go and how will we get there, but *also* specifically focuses on the internal capabilities that effort will require.

Just as outcome thinking itself is based upon certain tenets, so too does the Scorecard rest upon several fundamental assumptions. Perhaps more importantly, even though it was originally designed to apply to corporate structures, a careful reading will reveal the relevance of these foundationary statements to governmental and nonprofit organizations:

- *A clear strategic vision is not enough.* Echoing Drucker's criticism of a reliance upon mission to steer an organization, the catechism of BSC holds that even strategic vision, a set of long-term goals, is insufficient to guide an organization's actual operations.

- *Even when a strategic vision is in place, it typically has little or no impact on the immediate operating goals of departments and individuals.* Far too many day-to-day decisions and activities ignore the strategic plan. Again we are reminded of Drucker's observation that too often there is no operational design for translating mission into action. Into this vacuum often flow the everyday activities that consume many organizations' time and resources. Thus the BSC methodology states that the plan must be broken down into objectives and initiatives that have a direct relevance to the day-to-day activities of personnel and an organization's sub-units. Concrete ways must be devised for tying the strategic vision or mission goals of an organization to all the immediate goals and objectives of both individuals and departments. If those linkages cannot be demonstrated, the Scorecard tells us, the activities should not be allowed to continue.

- *Many organizations fail to collect the right information to monitor progress toward their strategic goals.* Too many organizations, focused primarily upon past performance, measure activity, whether human, mechanical or financial. They often fail to measure *capabilities*, the clearest measure of future success. The elusive task of *management* requires that the right data be gathered and *utilized* to provide effective measurement of objectives, but this is very often not done.

- *Most organizations do not identify or learn from their mistakes.* If an objective is not attained, it must be clearly understood which initiatives should be created to modify the objective or change the approach. Unfortunately, all too often the accustomed organizational response is to tinker with a failing approach or "try harder," rather than rethink the goals or design an entirely new approach.

In response to these needs, the BSC offers a 3-step program for redirecting organizational efforts and resource expenditures:

1. Identify the organization's strategic vision and the components of that strategy, its objectives, measures and initiatives
2. Separate the things the organization delivers (goods or services) from the things the organization *does*
3. Implement a strategy-focused organizational plan:
   - Translate strategy into operational terms everyone can understand
   - Link and align the organization around the strategy to create a "line of sight" from the boardroom to the front lines
   - Make strategy everyone's job through personal contribution to strategic implementation

- Make strategy a continuous process through organizational learning and adaptation
- Provide a change agenda for leadership at all organizational levels to mobilize change[57]

Within an organization, the BSC works at several levels. At a macro level, its use will allow for a realignment of an entire organization, redirecting the organization's many activities and resource expenditures toward its essential goals. Figure 6 depicts the ideal "balance" this achieves.

At a more discrete level, the Scorecard can be used successfully to monitor either a single program with several associated initiatives, or multiple programs within a specific organization. Utilizing the Scorecard's matrix system - perhaps one of the BSC's most important features - activities, initiatives, investments and dedicated resources can be matched to both long-term strategic goals and shorter-term milestones.

At a micro level, the matrix, called an "Initiative Map," can also be used to assess the capability of performance drivers to deliver the desired gains or objectives. Such a matrix may show an organization that it has one or more initiatives serving multiple objectives, a preponderance of initiatives serving a single objective, or objectives that have no initiatives supporting them at all.[58] This can be useful information to an organization attempting to align its efforts, resources and goals. For this reason, the BSC matrix can be used profitably to manage projects or undertakings involving more than one partner. Each participant's capabilities, resources, performance drivers and progress can be mapped and addressed. The Scorecard is certainly a powerful tool.

That said, however, there are some concerns regarding its use by government and nonprofit organizations.

Figure 6: The "balance" of the Balanced Scorecard[59]

While those offering training in BSC have in recent years adapted the model somewhat to fit the operating ecologies of governmental and nonprofit organizations, there is no escaping the model's corporate ancestry. In materials offered by even the leading trainers of the Scorecard, the parameters familiar to government and nonprofits appear grafted on, if they appear at all. Conversely, corporate concerns and language continue to appear throughout. Most specifically, the BSC does not yet appear to have evolved a sufficiently satisfying governmental or nonprofit substitute for the financial, bottom-line concerns that drive most corporate entities.

But even if this is merely a matter of materials not yet catching up with practice, there are three additional concerns that deserve attention. The first is the Scorecard's essential design for larger, more complex organizations. The very implementation of the Scorecard is envisioned to entail the successive involvement of three distinct "teams," the Core Team, the Leadership Team and various Sub- and Measurement Teams. For smaller organizations, the work of these "teams" in practice would fall on a single small group of managers.

A second concern revolves around the BSC concept of "breakthrough performance." For a nonprofit, and even more critically, for a governmental organization, what *is* "breakthrough performance"? *How* does this goal, defined by numerous variables in the corporate world, translate into the goals, culture and operating realities of governmental and nonprofit organizations? Arguably, the research on "high-performing" governmental or nonprofit organizations lags far behind comparable studies in the for-profit section, where works like Collins' and Porras' *Built to Last* regularly focus attention on the internal dynamics and attitudes that set leading corporate organizations apart.[60] Until these questions are answered, this core purpose of the Scorecard has questionable relevancy in non-corporate applications.

A final concern about the use of the BSC is the resource and leadership commitment needed to put its tool into practice. The comprehensive nature of the approach clearly requires executive level attention and the investment of financial and staffing resources that many governmental and nonprofit groups have difficulty allocating, particularly given the increased public scrutiny on government funding noted earlier.

These questions aside, there is no doubt that the Scorecard concept and certain of its aspects such as the *Initiative Map* can be extremely useful to the nonprofit and governmental sectors. Moreover, for complex programs or processes, there are few tools available to these organizations that can match the Scorecard's ability to capture the interconnectedness of initiatives, core capabilities, performance drivers and goals. The notion of aligning resources and activities to core, strategic goals is, likewise, an invaluable contribution of the BSC. Yet at the same time, the caution about the model's corporate roots should be borne in mind. Undoubtedly, additional research[61] and experience with application will smooth down some of the rough edges currently creating friction between the Scorecard's founding assumptions and its use in the governmental and nonprofit spheres. At this juncture, however, organizations in both realms should be advised to "handle with care."

Outcome Funding Framework

In the late 1980s, when Len Bickman was writing about core methodological issues in evaluation, he essentially argued that Outcome Thinking should be applied *before* a program or intervention was implemented...and way before the evaluation stage. His concern was that outcome-based evaluation was more difficult - and made little sense - if the program being evaluated had not been designed on an outcome basis. Little did Dr. Bickman know, however, that just at about the time he was making this groundbreaking suggestion, three men near Albany, New York, were about to go him one better and apply Outcome Thinking to the very funding process upon which human service programs traditionally depended. The three men were Hal Williams, President of The Rensselaerville Institute, Arthur Webb, then the Commissioner of the New York State Office of Mental Retardation and Developmental Disability, and William Phillips, at that time Program Development Bureau Chief with the NYS Department of Social Services.

It was their insight that, if clearly defined, verifiable outcomes were to be the target of human service programs, then fundamental changes had to take place in the perspectives of both those underwriting and those implementing the programs. For those supplying the financial support, Williams, Webb and Phillips suggested, there needed to be a shift from the perspective of a *funder*, whose primary interest is the distribution of money, to that of an *investor*, whose interest is in a *return*, defined by improvements in people's lives, on that investment...in other words, *results*.[62]

But there was also a shift prescribed for those receiving government funds - those implementing these programs. Too often, Williams argued, program targets were described, set and pursued in terms of *number of individuals served*, without addressing the "*so what*" question: "*So what* that 100 families were served? How many actually changed or improved in some way?"

Focusing on the number of clients served is an *activity* orientation, rather than an outcome focus. According to Williams' new vision, by contrast, the onus should be on the grantee to show not only that there was a need and that his/her organization had a plan for addressing it, but that the target, if achieved, will result in a tangible gain in the lives of some of those being served. This application of a return on investment perspective to social spending was a revolutionary concept in several regards. One clear implication was upon spending itself.

Until this point, *compliance* was the measure by which most social programs were judged: *did* a program meet the largely one-size-fits-all regulations that most funders (particularly government) had established as operating parameters? Were all mandated procedures followed? Were the correct reporting forms filled out and submitted? Was the money all accounted for? Were clients of the right economic, demographic and/or geographic profile?

Perhaps most significantly, many programs were assessed upon the basis of *how many* clients they served. From this came the concept of the "service unit," and the misleading accounting that placed a premium upon racking up the highest number of such units provided during the course of a funding cycle. But the only thing these measures gauged was *activity*; and in such a system, process becomes all, while results usually receive far less attention. When you fund *activity*, Williams, Webb and Phillips suggested, *activity* is usually all you get.

Looking at this system, they asked what if *any* of the traditional activity or compliance measures told grantors or program managers about what the programs were actually *accomplishing*.

The answer, they determined, was precious little. That led them to ask if this was any way to be determining whether a program ought to be funded. They decided that it was not.

Moreover, they came to recognize that, without information on what they called *human gain return*, budgets were the sole source for decision-making by funders. It was like being posed this question: *Is $20,000 a high price for an automobile?* The answer, of course, depends on the kind of vehicle, the shape it is in, how it was driven, etc. In other words it depends on what one is buying. In normal funding processes, the answer to the "What am I buying?" question was activity and process, rather than value and results.

Similarly, traditional funders did not differentiate an interest between buying *service* for a given population, as opposed to an interest in buying *change* in approaches and results. By introducing this concept, Williams and his colleagues showed the validity of results-based planning and decision-making for the social sector.

The funding decision should not be based upon rhetoric, commit-ment, devotion to a cause, or even promises of positive benefit. Rather, Williams, Webb and Phillips suggested, that decision should be based upon a potential grantee's ability to demonstrate a firm target, one that would produce verifiable benefits, and be achieved through the delivery of a *product* by a publicly focused individual or group of individuals with the energy and track record necessary to achieve these results. They called the concept *Outcome Funding* and suggested that its basis should not be the traditional human services *proposal*, but rather a *target plan*, that was much more akin to the business plan familiar to the corporate world. The comparison to conventional proposal formats was displayed as shown in Table 5.

Table 5: Proposal versus Target Plan[63]

The Proposal	The Target Plan
Needs Statement	Market & Customers
Goals & Objectives	Outcomes and Performance Targets
Project Description	The Product
Work Plan	Milestones
Staffing Plan	Key Individual
Credential of Proposing Group	Organizational Support
Evaluation Design	Verification
Line Item Budget	Financial Projections
Letters of Support	Customer Evidence

The realizations upon which these suggestions rested were the result of their combined real-world experience with state-funded programs that were *intended* to solve a wide variety of problems, but that often left everyone wondering whether they had, in fact, accomplished anything at all.

In place of this familiar, if frustrating system, Williams and company suggested that "an unambiguous statement of a performance target is an important prerequisite" for the achievement of goals.[64] This was a call for *all* parties concerned to be clear on what was being bought, funded and offered in human service programs. Beyond this, they also called for a shift from reliance upon evaluation, and towards *verification*. "Evaluation," they wrote, "measures *objectives*; but *verification* establishes the existence of *results*."[65] Put another way, they were arguing that a successful evaluation *might* show that a program had achieved its goals, but if the goals were activity-based, then real *results* might nonetheless remain unattained. Evaluation alone, as conventionally practiced, was not enough.

Core to the Outcome Funding Framework, as it became known, was the establishment of a vocabulary with precise definitions and a firm set of assumptions. Among the most important of these assumptions are the following:

- A partnership of investor and implementer is essential
- People, not plans (or even money) get things done
- Planning and doing are inseparable
- Success = results + learning

After five years of application, *Outcome Funding* evolved to the development of a parallel *Outcome Management* framework. While *Outcome Funding* applies the results standard to the process by which programs are designed, sold to underwriters, and funded, once a *target plan* is chosen for investment, *Outcome Management* helps programs apply outcome tools and perspectives to the accomplishment of those targets.

As with the Logic Model and other major outcome frameworks, *Outcome Management* begins with a series of "and then" statements (a variation upon the more familiar "if/then" statement) which detail the sequence of steps that lead to a desired performance target. But as opposed to the Logic Model, which uses these statements to describe the overall rationale for a program, *Outcome Management* insists that this sequence be used as a locational device to ensure that implementers know where they are in the desired chain of events.[66]

Progress toward the desired target is broken down into a series of *milestones*, the achievement of each being dependent upon those that preceded it in the sequence. Moreover, where traditional *activity* focuses upon what the *program* does, *milestones* focus upon what *customers* do, and how many do it *along the sequence*. The following example shows how this works. The shift in focus from agency action to customer reaction calls attention to the progress

Figure 7: Typical *Outcomes Management* funnel[67]

MILESTONES	NUMBER NEEDED	CONVERSION FACTOR
1. Call for information	400	
		4.0
2. Attend orientation and enroll	100	
		1.3
3. Attend 4 of 5 weekly workshops	75	
		2.5
4. Demonstrate learned skill	50	
		1.3
5. Attend 4 of 5 remaining work sessions	40	
		1.1
6. Retains information / skills from all sessions	35	
		1.0
7. Hired and starts job	34	
		1.1
8. Get satisfactory 30 day job assessment	30	
		1.5
9. Retained for 6 months	20	

the customer or client is making toward the desired changes, a crucial factor if *customer results* are to be achieved, measured and verified. Recognizing that many programs erroneously *assume* the interest and participation of clients, *Outcome Management* establishes as an early milestone the *actual* procurement of clients or customers.

Most often graphically depicted as a funnel, *Outcome Management* helps program implementers articulate the logic behind the program assumptions they make about how customers move from initial contact with a program to achieving the changes in condition, behavior or status that meets the criteria of success that have been identified and addressed. Figure 7 depicts a typical *Outcome Management* funnel.

This milestone graphic illustrates several key outcome elements. The first is the clearly established steps, or milestones, required to bring a set of customers to the desired target: retaining a job for six months. Milestones articulate the "and then"assumptions that underlay (or should) all programs. The second point relates to the target itself. Note that it goes beyond simply attendance at all sessions, or even graduation from the program. Targets in the Outcome Funding Framework, virtually always include an element of *retained benefit* for the client or customer. This concept of outcomes comes from the assumption that outcomes are first and foremost about what defines success. And in virtually all cases, when program leaders are asked to envision success, they stress some aspect of benefit that "takes" or goes beyond a one-time change.

A third piece of information contained in the milestone funnel relates to the quantitative aspects. The flow of numbers from top to bottom reflects the reality that virtually no enterprise, government, nonprofit or for-profit is successful with every customer or client with which it comes into contact. This attrition rate, the model suggests, is more realistic than the success rates of 100% (or even greater) than most conventional proposals project. Another way of reflecting customer flow is use of "conversion ratios" that offer a barometer illustrating the relationship between milestones. In this example, to get 20 clients to keep a job for 6 months, it takes 30 or 150% to be on the job for three months. Over time, by comparing the actual movement of clients with these assumptions, an increasingly accurate "calculus" of flow can be developed.

Milestones can quickly become valuable tools for program management, as they provide a real time test of the "and then" assumptions that are the core of program design. They reinforce the power of outcome thinking by pushing implementors to the end with the implicit "so what" sequence implied for each client step along the path. Where many programs begin with the notion of serving X number of clients, and then set out to find and enroll them, the *Outcome Funding / Management* model works backward from the desired number obtaining the final results, and, factoring in an attrition rate, suggests the actual number of recruits a program will need to meet this number. Attrition is a basic assumption of the model; hence the "funnel."[68]

But beyond allowing program *planners* to estimate how many individuals may drop out of a program at a given point (and therefore how many individuals they need to recruit to make the program a success), the graphic also allows program *managers* to ascertain if there are hidden drop off points they did not antici-pate. For example, if 50 rather than the 80 individuals anticipated to do so actually begin work, managers can immediately attempt to find out what happened. Were the jobs a mismatch to the interests of the clients or of their skills? Was location or trans-portation access a factor? Did the training assume skill levels that were absent? While the answers to these questions may not be obvious even after examination, the fact that they are considered moves most programs quantum steps closer to learning the answers.

The *Outcome Funding / Management* model has many strengths and applications within both programs and organizations. The uses cited as examples here do not adequately convey the potential of its *targets and milestones* core in functions ranging from program design to employee evaluation. Even where organizations are utilizing another Outcome Framework for their overall organizational management, this model can still be of great use when applied to specific programs.

At the same time, if the *Outcome Funding / Management* model has a weakness, it is in the degree to which organizations truly adopt its precepts. This model is significantly more involved than the Logic Model. It ultimately calls for deep-seeded changes in organizational thinking and procedures. Thus, it can sometimes come into conflict with organizational culture, history and practice. Where the Logic Model calls for organizations only to enunciate their theory of change (irrespective of whether it is flawed or unrealistic) and set forth an expected series of steps by which they will achieve their goals, the *Outcome Funding / Management* model implicitly challenges the very assumptions upon which a Logic approach is based.

The Logic Model rests almost exclusively upon a series of "if/then" statements. The *Outcome Funding / Management* model, by contrast, asks *HOW* the "if" will result in the "then." It is a more demanding approach, and not all organizations easily adapt to its rigors. For it to work, there is an intellectual and organizational change required, a mindset shift. Moreover, successfully applying the model is not enough if learning does not result and if changes or adaptations are not put in practice from its application.

In this regard, in the demands it places upon organizations, it is one of the more demanding outcome models available. As such, it requires a greater commitment of management energy and time resources than does the Logic Model, even though it can deliver vastly greater organizational gains. For detailed program planning and for attentive implementation, it is among the best prescriptions we have found. The question is whether it is a tonic all organizations will readily swallow.

Other Outcome Models

While the Logic Model, Balanced Scorecard and the Outcome Funding Framework are the best known and most widely used models; other models are in use, particularly in focused industries, and bear consideration.

Targeting Outcomes of Programs

A direct descendent of Bennett's hierarchy,[69] the TOP (**T**argeting **O**utcomes of **P**rograms) model was developed by Claude Bennett and Kay Rockwell in 1994.[70] Initially geared toward agricultural extension services, the model appears to be primarily used in rural areas where it is well regarded. TOP includes a practical hierarchy for targeting outcomes, tracking progress toward achieving targets, and evaluating the degree to which programs impact targeted conditions.

As might be expected given its parentage, TOP is based primarily upon a hierarchy that integrates program evaluation within the program development process, and focuses on outcomes in planning, implementing, and program evaluation. It relies upon this framework to target specific outcomes, and then to assess the degree to which the outcome targets are reached.[72] It helps managers answer four basic questions:

1. Why have a program?
2. How should the program be conducted?
3. Has the program design been implemented?
4. What are the benefits the program delivered?

Utilizing a form of Bennett's original hierarchy, TOP uses the graphic in Figure 8 to depict its seven constituent levels. It is presumed by the model that most information, education, and training programs can be represented by the two-sided, seven-level hierarchy, with each of the hierarchy's levels containing a number of additional assumptions. Program development is depicted by descending the model on the left-hand side; program performance is depicted by ascending the model on the right-hand side.

Figure 8: Seven constituent levels of the TOP Model[71]

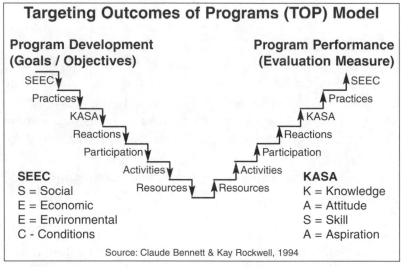

Targeting Outcomes of Programs (TOP) Model

Program Development (Goals / Objectives)

Program Performance (Evaluation Measure)

SEEC
Practices
KASA
Reactions
Participation
Activities
Resources

SEEC
Practices
KASA
Reactions
Participation
Activities
Resources

SEEC
S = Social
E = Economic
E = Environmental
C - Conditions

KASA
K = Knowledge
A = Attitude
S = Skill
A = Aspiration

Source: Claude Bennett & Kay Rockwell, 1994

At Level 1, SEE represents social, economic, and environmental conditions (or situations) that may need improvement. At Level 2, *practices* are considered to be patterns of behaviors, procedures, or actions that influence SEE condition. Through educational programs, it is anticipated that individuals, groups, organizations, and communities will adopt practices and technologies that achieve needed SEE outcomes. These practices are adopted as program participants apply relevant knowledge, attitudes, skills, and aspirations (KASA) measures.

At Level 3, KASA characteristics are seen to influence the adoption of selected practices and technologies to help achieve targeted social, economic, and environmental outcomes.[73] Changes in KASA can occur when people react positively to their involvement in program activities. At Level 4, *reactions* reflect participants' degree of positive or negative interest in topics addressed in the program, their acceptance of activity leaders and their attraction to the educational methods. Delivering relevant, research-based subject matter can help hold clientele interest. People may obtain information, education, or assistance from different agencies or organizations at the same time. Thus, the way they react to an activity sponsored by one organization may be influenced by complementary activities that are sponsored by other agencies or organizations.

At Level 5, program participants may include individuals, families, groups, organizations, or communities. Participants must be sufficiently involved in program activities to acquire KASA and adopt practices needed to improve SEE conditions. Duration, continuity, frequency, and intensity of program participation all contribute to the amount of KASA change. The *activities* envisioned in Level 6 are the various educational strategies and events used to inform, educate, or train target audiences. They can range from direct personal contacts to indirect technological or mass media approaches. Program activities are determined by requirements to obtain positive reactions from participants as well as other factors needed to achieve desired changes in KASA and practices. Program activities are supported by program resources.

Finally, at Level 7, *resources* are the time, money, and staff (including volunteers) used to plan, promote, implement, and evaluate programs. Resources might also include research-based educational materials, organizational maintenance, communication technologies, and transportation.[74]

It is worth noting that, as a true outcome model, TOP also follows Schwitzer's typology of outcomes, tracking immediate, intermediate and long-term outcomes separately, and it contains the explicit notion of a feedback loop for learning.

Another interesting aspect of TOP is that, in its evaluation phase, it breaks down the exercise into three distinct activities: process evaluation, outcome evaluation and impact evaluation. The model also suggests that these three aspects can be undertaken independently of one another:

- Process evaluation examines the extent to which a program is operating as it was intended.
- Outcome evaluation assesses the extent to which a program's outcome-oriented objectives are achieved.
- Impact evaluation looks at the net effect of a program by comparing program outcomes with no-program baseline, an estimate of what would have happened in the absence of the program.[75]

A key strength of TOP is that it helps integrate program development and program evaluation; program implementers and managers can use the same concepts in program development as they do in program evaluation.[76]

TOP appears to be fairly easy to use, although some practitioners may be tempted to skip some of the steps of its hierarchy. While it should be considered by a wide range of human service organizations, its clearly agricultural roots and primary application could prove off-putting to more urban communities and programs. They are encouraged, however, to look past this image and give the model serious thought. It is easy to use, fully functional as an outcome model, can be discretely applied and does not necessarily ask for an organizational mind-set shift. At the same time, its hierarchy allows for more incremental program planning than some other more widely known models, and it incorporates an evaluation phase even in its earliest stages. Urban-based nonprofit organizations are certainly urged to give this model a fair examination; it could prove to be a most useful tool.

Managing for Results

Managing for Results (MFR) is a public sector-oriented outcome methodology that focuses on defining and then achieving results that are important to government and its stakeholders. Some observers suggest that MFR is more of an *approach* to governmental operations than it is an actual outcome *system*.[77]   Indeed, it is not uncommon for a governmental organization employing MFR to include another recognized outcome system *within* the overall MFR framework.[78] But this matter of semantics aside, proponents believe that, by following the precepts of MFR, the organization develops a shared, widely understood framework, using performance measurement for: a) setting goals and objectives, b) managing, c) allocating resources, and d) evaluating its accomplishments. In this, it is close enough to an example of Outcome Thinking to warrant inclusion here. By way of example, the National Governors Association defines MFR as including the following components:

- Results-based budgeting and allocation of resources that directs investments to strategies that achieve desired outcomes
- Program evaluation to identify best practices, determine cause-and-effect relationships, and measure impacts. Continuous improvement processes that benchmark performance and promote adoption of best practices to achieve desired results
- The use of indicators and measures of performance to demonstrate accountability and develop public trust;
- Performance monitoring or auditing to verify outcomes and validate measures[79]

Largely driven at the federal level by GPRA and recent statements by the Governmental Accounting Standards Board (GASB), MFR has also been adopted by local governments as a way of fulfilling government's duty to be publicly accountable and to enable the public to assess that accountability.[80] The model's popularity has not only spread to state and local governments throughout the U.S., but has also been adopted as national policy in Canada.[81]

One of the tools used in Managing for Results is the concept of *service efforts and accomplishment* measures (SEA). GASB has issued guidance in the development, use and reporting of these SEA measures in a series of research reports collectively entitled *Service Efforts and Accomplishments Reporting: Its Time Has Come*.[82] This report defines performance measurement and applies these concepts to twelve government functions including elementary and secondary education, health, road maintenance, higher education, economic development, mass transit, police, fire, water and waste water, sanitation, hospitals, and public assistance, and details types of performance measures as follows:

- Input Indicators - monetary and non-monetary resources
- Output Indicators - the amount of services provided
- Efficiency Indicators - the relationship of input indicators to output indicators
- Outcome Indicators - the impact on the customer
- Explanatory Data - a variety of information relevant to a service that helps users to understand the factors affecting it[83]

As with other Outcome Thinking systems, a major component of Managing For Results is the notion of using performance data for managerial purposes. In MFR, the idea centers on two questions:

- How do we know if the government and its programs are effective?
- How do we know if the government and its programs are efficient?

In application and practice by governmental and nonprofit organizations, MFR resembles the Balanced Scorecard more that it does other familiar outcome models, in that one of its primary foci is the alignment of resources with desired goals.[84] While this is implicit in all outcome models, it is particularly accented in BSC, MFR and a few other models that have more of a clear-cut business, or fiscal accountability component.

Also separating MFR from more traditional outcome models is the fact that its specific *theory of change* is rarely expressed or even depicted. Constituent processes and variables are accounted for in detail, but their interaction, causal relationships and influences upon each other and upon the desired goal are left to the user's imagination. In fact, it might not be going too far to say that MFR does not contain a requirement for a theory of change to be specifically articulated. For nonprofit entities seeking to influence a problem or social condition, this can not only be a danger, but belies the entire reason for which outcome modeling was conceived in the first place.

In sum, while Managing For Results may be an important part of a governmental or nonprofit organization's *overall* strategy toward a results orientation, increased accountability and verified outcomes, it is probably not a strong enough tool to replace a more traditional outcome model. This is especially true where MFR leaves unaddressed the issues of specifically *how* desired outcomes will be achieved. It is a good *context* within which to place and use a more traditional outcome framework, but by itself it probably cannot offer a nonprofit, service organization the guiding parameters that will lead to success.

Getting To Outcomes

While other variations exist,[85] the most widely recognized version of the Getting to Outcomes concept is a nominally outcome-based model sponsored by the Center for Substance Abuse Prevention (CSAP) through its National Center for the Advancement of Prevention (NCAP).[86] Originally commissioned through NCAP, development of the model began with the work of Drs. Wandersman, Chinman and Imm at the University of South Carolina.[87]

Aimed at local provider agencies, the model is intended to lead participants through an "empowerment evaluation model" (providing specific skills and user-friendly tools), incorporating basic elements of program planning, implementation, evaluation, and sustainability. It assumes that these agencies want to make a difference in the lives of children and families in their communities, that the agencies' funders want them to be accountable, and that the agencies want to show that their programs work. Getting to Outcomes is suggested as a way to meet these goals.[88]

The program leads agency managers and planners through 10 questions, each built around a specific focus that is intended to incorporate the basic elements of program planning, implementation, evaluation, and sustainability:

1. Needs/Resources: What underlying needs and resources must be addressed?
2. Goals: What are the goals, target population, and objectives (i.e., desired outcomes)?
3. Best Practice: Which science- (evidence-) based models and best practice programs can be useful in reaching the goals?
4. Fit: What actions need to be taken so the selected program "fits" the community context?
5. Capacities: What organizational capacities are needed to implement the program?
6. Planning: What is the plan for this program?

7. <u>Process Evaluation</u>: Does the program have high implementation fidelity?
8. <u>Outcome Evaluation</u>: How well is the program working?
9. <u>Quality Improvements</u>: How will continuous quality improvement strategies be included?
10. <u>Sustainability</u>: If the program is successful, how will it be sustained?

Getting to Outcomes uses a logic model as its basis, defining that model as "a series of connections that link problems or needs you will be addressing, with the actions you will take to obtain your outcomes."[89] It also introduces users to the concept of the logic model's familiar "if-then" statements, to an outline of the notion of a theory of change, and to the idea of accountability. However, while more in-depth training and direction may be available elsewhere, the primary Getting to Outcomes guidebook, at least, offers little substantive information on any of these concepts.

The model *does* however, make clear the difference between outcomes and outputs, and the fact that a particular program's objective must express the result of agency action, not level of effort.[90] Similarly, it clearly delineates between program objectives and measurable target goals, and suggests that these be measured according to familiar BACKS or KASA standards. In sum, it has most of the characteristics of a traditional outcome model.

If Getting to Outcomes is to be faulted in any way, it is in the fact this popular version of it was obviously developed with a *specific* application, substance abuse prevention, in mind. Most available information on the model focuses much attention upon the *process* of intervention development and implementation. Outcome Thinking, as such, is given proportionately less attention when compared with *overall* program capabilities.

The "logic" of the program's logic model is given little attention in the overall scheme of things. Meanwhile, such considerations as diverse community stakeholder involvement, cultural appropriateness and intervention "fit" are given considerable stress. The "how to" steps of program initiation are similarly given considerable attention, and numerous checklist forms are provided to monitor fidelity to the program. These are not failings of a model for program development; however, they leave the Outcome Thinking involved largely to assumption and intuition.

This said, the model has nonetheless been adapted to evaluations of youth empowerment programs [91] to therapeutic recreation intervention programs[92] and is cited as a broadly applicable example of program development and evaluation.[93] In the absence of any more formalized training in Outcome Thinking, Getting to Outcomes is a useful tool that many local nonprofit organizations can use, learn from and adapt to their particular needs and circumstances.

Scales and Ladders

Scales and Ladders (S&L) is a matrix-based outcome system most popularly associated with the implementation of the Results Oriented Management and Accountability (ROMA) system instituted as a result of the federal GPRA of 1993, primarily within Community Services Block Grant (CSBG)-funded programs.

ROMA is intended to be an approach to management that builds accountability into the activities organizations, a way for them to evaluate the effectiveness of their programs and make improvements in agency capacity and performance. But ROMA is also the common language for members of the nation's Community Action Network, and it was this connection that led to the widespread popularity of Scales and Ladders.

In August of 1994, Donald Sykes, the Director of the Office of Community Services (OCS), chartered the Community Services Block Grant Monitoring and Assessment Task Force (MATF). The task force created six broad goals and a list of direct measures for members of the Community Action Network to use when responding to GPRA. Under federal legislation, states are free to devise their own ROMA implementation systems and, in an effort to offer some guidance in this, MATF organized a ROMA Scales and Ladders Committee. Over the course of five years, the Committee, in cooperation with leading consultants and representatives of the Community Action Network around the country, decided upon the technology of "scales" as one of the best means for meeting the mandates of ROMA.[94]

The model's essential concept centers around a series of scales and their placement within a sequence of matrices.[95] A *scale* is defined as a continuum that describes different states or conditions of status. It has a beginning point and an ending point, with increments in between. Both points can be defined fairly arbitrarily; what *is* required, however, is an internal logic that links the scales into a sequential order. The steps on the scale are defined by *indicators*, factors or variables that describe the condition classified by the scale. There are three types of indicators:

- Mutually Exclusive Indicator
- Multiple Indicators
- Floating Indicators

The increments between the scales do not have to be of equal value like those on a thermometer. Instead, they can represent a logarithmic scale, as the Richter Scale does, in which the units of measure get progressively larger by multiplying instead of adding. The decision concerning the value of the scale increments is entirely up to the organization creating the scale, and there is no magic number of thresholds that make one scale any more desirable than another. Similarly, the indicators for the levels are defined by the organization to fit the particular program. The rationale for this is that the model is not intended to aggregate the *progress* on the scales or the *progress on the scale thresholds* as the definitive test of a program's success. Rather, a scale is made up of individual data pieces that, <u>together</u>, tell a complete story; it is the portrait presented by the *whole*, rather than the discrete data points, that comprise the model's value.[96] The measures are not absolute, nor are they intended to be. Instead, the model is an instrument that is used to place a client, a community, or a program on a continuum. It is used to show incremental *and relative* progress, stabilization, or decline in a situation.

As utilized in ROMA, scales are categorized as applying to individuals or families, communities, or organizations.[97] Table 6 typifies an S&L matrix, this one applied to "equity" (equality) measures in a community.

The model is reminiscent of BSC in its use of a matrix, but instead of tracking initiatives against targets, as in the BSC resource alignment, Scales and Ladders tracks *progress* against targets. For example, instead of judging that a family's condition is "self-sufficient" or "not self-sufficient," S&L measures the family on a scale of 1 to 5, (*in-crisis, vulnerable, safe, stable, or thriving*) relative to the goal of self-sufficiency. In other words, it measures a family's *degree* or *level* of self-sufficiency, and over time hopefully shows progress as a result of the program or intervention. The scale is applied to a situation primarily at two specific points, at in-take and during follow-up (although one or more mid-term assessments are theoretically possible). The basic pre- and post-tests enable the organization to see the degree to which the customer's situation has changed.

The strengths of the S&L model include the following:

• The model consists of a series of related scales grouped

Table 6: Typical Sales and Ladders matrix[98]

THRESHOLD		EQUITY SCALE
5.	Thriving	The community understands the strengths inherent in diversity, celebrates **differences** and, therefore, is committed to the development and maintenance of a healthy socioeconomic and demographic mix. The appreciation of diversity has led to establishment **of equal treatment and opportunity** as the prevailing norms in both economic and social transactions in the community. All cultures and ethnic groups are working together for the common good.
4.	Safe	Knowledge and understanding of culture and customs of various groups represented in the community's population are common throughout the community. That knowledge has bred an understanding that differing customs and values can coexist and a sensitivity to and appropriate accommodation of those varied customs and values. **Affirmation** of the rights and the values of others, despite differences, is the norm.
3.	Stable	Members of the community are generally **aware** of differences among the populations present in the community. An atmosphere of **tolerance** prevails with little or no inter-group conflict. There is a growing awareness of the importance of understanding and community among diverse populations.
2.	Vulnerable	Diverse populations are generally isolated from one another and are **uninformed** regarding the customs, values, history and contributions of the other populations residing in the community. There is a general sense of complacency regarding lack of interaction and communication among various groups. Lack of understanding and consequent insensitivity are commonplace.
1.	In crisis	**Fear and conflict** characterize interactions among diverse populations. Various populations are consistently working at cross-purpose. Open hostility is common.

together in a matrix. When combined, these scales can be used to tell a larger story.

- Scales can be used to measure concepts that are not easily quantified. Organizations are using scales to gauge progress toward economic self-sufficiency, degree of agency development, amount of community investment, and other concepts that are otherwise difficult to measure. Scales allow organizations to assign values to easily identified, discrete conditions, and to combine these values into a single measure of a complex idea like self-sufficiency.

- Scales allow organizations to measure intermediate steps. By comparing scale results taken at two different times, one can determine how much short-term progress has been made toward a long-term goal such as self-sufficiency. Agencies using scales can demonstrate multiple interim successes even when the ultimate goal may not have been achieved. Agencies can thereby provide periodic motivation to all the stakeholders, such as the clients, the staff, and the funding sources.

- Although it may be cumbersome to do so, scales allow each client's path to be tracked separately. Through scales, each improvement of an agency's capacity can be seen separately, and each development in a community effort can be shown individually.

A question remains, however, as to whether Scales and Ladders is a true outcome system, or whether it is actually more of a tracking system.

Like other outcome models, S&L does track *outcomes*. The system does not depict activities, but rather the effect those activities have upon a situation. It also contains a powerful learning component because it offers a clear picture of where a program's progress may have stalled: if progress significantly stops in enough cases at a certain point on "the ladder," managers can clearly see that there is a problem. Moreover, as noted, it shows progress *even where program completion was not achieved*. For reasons described previously, this is an important quality shared by the best of the various outcome models.

But at the same time, there are characteristics of S&L that differentiate it from other outcome models. It does not, for example, rest upon the demonstration of a valid theory of change. Through its scales, it does imply the accomplishments that would move a subject to the next highest scale, but it does not prescribe a course of action to get to that next level. Like a thermometer, the model doesn't tell you what you need to do to change your temperature or improve your condition; it just tells you what your temperature is. Even in its assessments that result in placement in a certain scale on the ladder, judgments are sometimes objective and sometimes subjective. The assessment is not absolute, and the findings therefore remain "soft."

Without question, Scales and Ladders is an important tool that can be used profitably by both nonprofit and governmental organizations, particularly as an *evaluation* tool. But it is only one weapon in the arsenal of accountability. While the ability to use it well is a valuable survival skill in the era of outcomes, by itself it may not be sufficient to bring true Outcome Thinking to an organization's internal or external operations.

Results Mapping

Results Mapping, developed a decade ago by Dr. Barry Kibel and disseminated through the Results Mapping Laboratory of the Pacific Institute for Research and Evaluation,[99] is an outcome based evaluation tool that attempts to answer the question of how to systematically capture the richness often contained in the otherwise non-quantifiable anecdotal evidence many programs have available.

The debate over the value and use of anecdotal evidence has gone on since the birth of the modern outcome movement in the 1990s. The central question of this debate has been whether all important outcomes are quantifiable, and whether those that are not should be included in an organization's evidence of successfully achieved outcomes.

Within both the outcome community and the larger nonprofit world, anecdotal and empirical information are seen as not only quite distinct from one another, but also of completely different natures, with anecdotal information appearing to many observers to be of decidedly less intrinsic value. Many believe, for example, that empirical data is more "reliable" than anecdotal information, primarily because of the way it is collected and reported. This attraction is compounded by the fact that the often-unsubstantiated nature of anecdotal information is seen as a severe handicap to the wide acceptance of it as an accurate measure of progress or accomplishment. In addition:

- *Anecdotal information is generally not collected according to an established set of criteria, or seeking an agreed-upon body of knowledge.* Rather, when it comes to anecdotal evidence, many nonprofit organizations make little or no attempt to proactively gather this information. Instead, many use whatever anecdotal information comes their way.

- *Haphazardly collected anecdotal information very often lacks standards and common threads that would allow it to be put together to form a cohesive, coherent argument.* Compounding this, lacking a formal, agreed-upon structure, even when the stories are complete and accurate, the styles of relating them will vary greatly across storytellers, and therefore aspects accentuated are different.

- *Many nonprofits tell the wrong stories for the wrong reason.* As currently utilized, the attraction of most anecdotal information is largely emotional, and the evidence is often presented in the wrong way: as now collected, the actors in such stories, rather than the intervention processes and the gains they achieved, are often accentuated. Organizations often fail, in the presentation of their anecdotal information, to remember that the point of the stories is not the details of the stories themselves, but rather the larger truths the organization wishes to illustrate.

* *Anecdotal information is often not verified.*

In short, what has been lacking is a tool that allows organizations to successfully capture, standardize and utilize this important resource. Results Mapping is designed to be one approach toward answering that need.

The basic idea behind the model is to lay out in sequential form the essential interventions, the reactions and the milestones achieved as a result of a program. If this is done for an organization's "top few" stories, Dr. Kibel contends, organizations can demonstrate their successes and full worth to funders, board members, and others.

Results Mapping is used to capture key facts, score, analyze, and provide feedback to improve the best work that a program does with its clients, be they individuals, families, teams, groups, communities, organizations, or systems. Based upon select client "stories," each story should feature some of the best work a program does. It is not the client's life story that is being presented. Nor is it only the interaction between the program with the client. Rather, the design rests upon a story that begins with the first interaction between the program and the client, and extends to further program-client interactions, to program interactions with the client's support system, to client interchanges with others mobilized by the program to assist the client, and to personal client achievements in support of self or to benefit others.[100]

An important difference between Results Mapping and more traditional outcome systems, however, becomes clear when Kibel's rationale for the entire exercise is examined. The best of outcome thinking lends itself to program planning, to program and organizational management, as well as to evaluation. Results Mapping, by contrast, focuses primarily upon evaluation and, moreover, views the validation - if not the celebration - of "the hard and sometimes outstanding work of program staff in making these outcomes more likely" as of equal importance.

Results Mapping also differs from more traditional models in its insistence that only the "best" stories be included in the map-based evaluation. Kibel believes that these "best success" stories contain examples of everything the program is doing right, of examples and ways in which staff went above and beyond the call of duty, and that they offer a pattern to be emulated. While this may be true enough, the logic can be questioned. In his reliance upon "success stories," Kibel apparently ignores the cases where a few sterling successes might mask a much larger number of near misses or even outright programmatic failures. He seems to dismiss the fact that one of the most common specific complaints against the use of anecdotal evidence - particularly the exclusive use of such evidence - is that this approach all but insures that funders and other stakeholders will receive only positive, "success stories," leaving stories of lesser success, often the most enlightening, unaddressed. How, it might be asked, are problems to be addressed if they are not identified and confronted? Kibel, however, does not answer this question, preferring instead to suggest that by modifying the old, familiar "activity" stories to include the results to which those activities led, the examples worthy of imitation found within success stories can be identified, celebrated and repeated.

The Results Mapping tool is a somewhat radical approach when seen against most traditional outcome models. It does not track outcomes, does not rely upon objective, measurable variables, is not designed for program or organizational planning, and is a subjective management tool.

Much like Scales and Ladders, Results Mapping is more of a tracking device than it is an actual outcome model. In this case, Results Mapping tracks interventions that contribute to the constituent milestones of a desired outcome. More specifically, through its reliance upon stories, Results Mapping allows for the capture and analysis of the more individualized and subjective aspects of an intervention. This is not without value.

It is also true that, by attempting a standardized approach to the use of anecdotal evidence, Results Mapping represents a useful contribution to the effort to find replicable information in these stories. All programs have these stories. But as we have said, many organizations do not know how to use them to full advantage; too many wind up just being a sidebar or photo caption in a newsletter. Because Results Mapping focuses upon the key intervention points in a story, it offers a way to avoid getting lost in the drama and human interest details that many organizations often mistake as the stories' primary value.

Results Mapping is not a true outcome model. But, if properly used, it can be a useful tool for organizations that want to go beyond numbers and use the many stories their files contain.

Results-based Accountability (RBA)

This model, also called *Results and Performance Accountability*, was primarily designed by Mark Friedman[101] of the Fiscal Policy Study Institute.[102] Emulating Covey, the system approaches a situation by starting with desired ends and working backward toward the means to achieve them. The RBA model first describes what a desired result would look like, defines that result in measurable terms, and uses those measures to gauge success or failure.

Designed to be a real-time approach that an organization can rapidly implement, the goal of Friedman's model suggests that programs and agencies quickly identify their three or four most important success measures, making sure that these measures focus on customer results, and not just on the amount of effort expended. Thereafter, he suggests that they create baselines for these measures, and hold themselves and their managers account-able for making progress against their baselines. His model envisions using these measures in a simple day-to-day manage-ment process that builds data-based decision making into the culture of the organization, and also produces information needed for the budget.

The RBA model rests upon asking - and answering - three basic questions: What do we want? How will we recognize it? What will it take to get there? To answer these questions, RBA suggests the following focus:

- Results: What conditions of well-being, stated in plain language, do we want for children, adults, families and communities?
- Experience: How do we experience these results in our everyday lives?
- Indicators: How could we recognize these conditions in measurable terms?
- Baselines: Where have we been and where are we headed on the indicators?
- Story behind the baselines: Why do these indicator baselines look the way they do? What are the causes?
- Partners: Who are the potential partners who have a role to play in doing better?

- Strategy: What works? What do we think it will take to do better?
- Action plan and budget: What do we propose to actually do?

The model also includes three important precepts designed to help ensure the achievement of a program's desired results. The first is data-driven, results-based decision-making. All decisions, the system says, should be based upon the use of desired results as the starting point, and all decisions should be made in light of their contribution to desired goals. Reminiscent of corporate alignment strategies, this strongly implies that ancillary considerations may often distract an organization and hamper the chances for successfully reaching organizational or programmatic goals. Similarly, results-based budgeting, another familiar corporate tool, is the model's recommended form of fiscal decision making, an approach that uses desired results to steer the development of budgets. According to RBA, this concept should be applied to budgets for programs and for organizations.

The third foundation concept of RBA is Performance Accountability, or the accountability of managers to stakeholders, for the performance of a program, agency or service system. It involves identifying the most important performance measures for programs and agencies, and holding managers accountable for doing a good job on those measures.

At this point, RBA makes a significant distinction between what it calls "population accountability" and "program or agency accountability." Maintaining that these are two profoundly different types of accountability that often get erroneously mixed together, the model treats them separately. In the RBA view, accountability for population well-being cannot be assigned to any one person or organization. Where numerous actors are involved, it is by definition a shared responsibility. Program and agency accountability, on the other hand, can be assigned to the manager of the program or agency.

Separating these two accountability lines allows for a program's impact to be assessed irrespective of progress (or lack of progress) made toward the larger goal shared by other organizations or programs. By separating program accountability from population accountability, the RBA model allows each organization involved in a shared goal to be judged on its own merits. It removes at least one impulse to assign blame and, when all parties agree that more needs to be done to accomplish a common goal, it strengthens a community's sense of collective responsibility.

One of the RBA's most distinguishing characteristics is its inclusion of the "Crosswalk," a tool for matching RBA with other outcome models. With the growing number of different outcome models now available, it is not uncommon for a large organization to have two or more separate departments using different models. It is also not uncommon for managers and staff to have prior experience with one or more models different than the one their organization might currently be using. How do these different models relate to one another? Do some have characteristics that others lack? Is one more appropriate to a given point in the life of an organization or program? While no one graphic can answer all these questions, RBA utilizes the Crosswalk as a way to analyze differences between it and other frameworks.

Using Crosswalk, it is possible to see where one framework is more complete than another, or where one uses a different thinking process for the same set of ideas. By utilizing the Crosswalk form,[103] organizations can plug in the characteristics of any outcome models to obtain at least a rough idea of how they resemble and differ from one another. This will not answer all questions regarding the utility of one model over another in a given situation, but it can prove to be a useful guide to organizations seeking a basic understanding of the differences between models.

The RBA model is a thorough, outcome-oriented template for an organization looking for a real-time implementation plan for a results-based intervention. Based upon significant research and experience,[104] its web-based presentation is thorough, accessible and understandable. With a heavy emphasis on actual implementation, it literally walks practitioners through the often confusing steps of setting goals and working toward them.

If there are any caveats regarding the model, they are these: Although designed to be a disciplined approach to outcomes, one that stresses the need for reliance upon available research and data, the model's parallel accent on getting started quickly might tempt an organization to move too quickly on the implementation of a program or intervention before all the necessary questions are asked and answered. In similar fashion, the model does not overly emphasize a real examination of a program's theory of change, the logic of what it is doing in relation to what it hopes to achieve. Although Friedman personally believes that this *is* stressed in the RBA guide, more of an unmistakable focus on the importance of the concept would strengthen the model and practitioners' application of it. These notes aside, however, RBA remains a very useful approach to results-based implementation, one that any organization should certainly consider adopting.

WHAT'S NEXT

Given this discussion of the roots of the "outcome movement" along with an assessment of its current state, the logical next questions are about the future. Is the "movement" near the end of its natural lifecycle, poised to join the history of similar "movements" that have struck the public sector, once-popular ideas like Zero Based Budgeting and TQM? Or, is there a different future ahead? Is it here to stay - to evolve to a new a better level? And if so, what forms might this new level take?

We offer some modest perspectives on these questions, including some assessment of their likelihood. We close with more of a wish than a prediction, using the power of outcome *thinking* to describe a preferred future...preferred, at least by these observers.

Three Likely Scenarios

There are three scenarios that seem likely to be in the offing for the "outcome movement". These are in no way mutually exclusive, nor are they offered in the order of their likelihood or importance.

Tightening the grip. Driven largely by government demands for increased accountability and the other forces described earlier, and particularly in response to the financial strains placed on government during the 2000-2002 period, the expansion of result and performance based budgeting and contracting approaches is likely to continue to gain traction. This accountability-driven orientation, which directly connects program outcomes to cost and payments, has recently gained credibility with those who control government spending. This has happened even though the experience of several performance-based budgeting approaches has been, at best, uneven.[105]

Several large international organizations including the United Nations and its affiliate groups, like the World Health Organization and the World Food Programme have recently launched major Results-based Budgeting (RBB) initiatives. Domestically, the Federal government, under the auspice of the GPRA, has been the impetus for new outcome-based funding approaches in such areas as services to persons with HIV and AIDS. As the US economy seems to be emerging from a prolonged slowdown, it will be interesting to see whether the pay-for-performance emphasis abates. We believe it will not, at least for the near term, given the predictable delay the public sector typically experiences as the economy turns. Also, with the significant increase in deficit spending, a reduced interest in cost control seems highly unlikely. The challenge will remain, however, in successfully enabling conventionally budget based entities like large government to easily shift to a performance based atmosphere that avoids a distinctly punitive flavor.

Into the tool chest. Another possibility is that outcome-based thinking and its associated frameworks become one of a number of tools and techniques which are selectively employed by government, philanthropy and the nonprofit sectors in a wide range of forms. By being one of a number of tools to enable improved performance, pluralism is clearly served and market forces are enabled, thus promoting the evolution of the most effective and efficient approaches. We believe that this scenario will develop in parallel with the tightening of accountability pressures described above. The likelihood that these essentially opposite forces could increase the conflict between funder and service provider is clearly possible - with the ferocity of this conflict largely dependent on how tight public and philanthropic funding becomes.

The Technology Connection. A focus on results is significantly increasing the recognition by government, philanthropy and nonprofit groups of the importance of timely and accurate information to confirm outcome accomplishment. Without the dramatic improvements in information technology, it is highly unlikely that the outcome movement would be as vibrant as it is today. Just as the connection between outcomes and money is being strengthened, so to, in our judgment, will be the nexus of outcomes and electronically collected and reported information. Again spurred by Federal requirements, a number of national programs are recognizing that use of an effective outcome framework can only come about if reliable information is available. The rapid developments in technology, particularly with the advent of the Internet, will continue to be a potent force for change and evolution in the outcome arena as elsewhere. There is also significant possibility that smaller agencies will be unable or unwilling to make the investments, in personnel, training and machines, necessary to enable them to compete in an increasingly outcome oriented world.

Morphing into the Next Movement. A final possibility is that free standing outcome approaches like the Logic Model or our own Outcome Funding Framework either directly evolves or is subsumed into a broader systemic model of organizational change. The recent interest in the *Balance Scorecard* by the Federal government may be suggestive of this development. In one nonprofit agency we know, an eight year commitment to outcome management has led it to a fascinating relationship with General Electric's Six Sigma quality control framework, with a goal of creating a seamless integration between the two.

In a similar vein, this examination of the strengths and applications of the major outcome models has led us to the conclusion that elements of a number of these models might be combined to create a more powerful and broadly applicable product. Discussions are currently underway about launching a prototype to test this assumption.

A Vision for the Future

We end with an attempt to apply outcome thinking to the outcome movement itself. How can we in good faith preach the power of outcomes and not practice it in our consideration of its future?

And so here is our attempt to "play the outcome game" and answer this question:

> *What would the ideal application of outcome thinking in the "social sector" look like? What would be different, what would be better, what would people be saying or doing that defines success?*

1. The language of outcomes is firmly established in the public lexicon. While a variety of terms are used, the core distinctions between outputs, outcomes and impacts are widely accepted and employed. Universities would teach it, agencies would use it, communication would be greatly improved.

2. The benefits for those served are paramount in most conversations. An examination of all public programs, new or ongoing, would center on the outcome question:

   > *How many people benefited, and how does that compare with what was projected?*

3. Government, philanthropy, and the nonprofit groups that rely on them, act as true partners - recognizing that their relationship is a symbiotic one - each party dependent on the other for success. Finger pointing is greatly reduced and cross agency knowledge transfer is valued and widely employed.

4. Discussions of what worked and, most importantly, what didn't, would be commonplace and honest. Funders and political leaders would seek to understand before passing judgment.

5. Direct service groups and those that support them will dedicate modest resources (about 5% of total program costs) to verify or confirm outcome accomplishment. Gone are the complaints that "evaluation funds" only reduce the number of those served.

6. Outcome-relevant data is inexpensively available and, while protected on confidentiality grounds, is seen as valid and reliable.

7. Staff, at all levels of the system, embraces an outcome orientation because it helps them understand the purpose of their work, what they are accomplishing and how to improve their practice.

8. Outcome assessments lead to the development and spreading of improved program practices. Organizational learning is a coveted investment and is directly connected with personal and professional development. The outcome focus is widely seen as enhancing the working environment of public and social sector work even without a significant increase in salaries.

9. Funding decisions clearly take into account past outcome accomplishments and these decisions are widely seen as fair and equitable by those who receive the funds, those who don't, and those who make the decisions.

While admittedly ambitious and, even highly optimistic, we suggest this vision as a powerful way to motivate and energize the thousands of people of good will who work in these fields. And while attainability is uncertain, we firmly believe in the adage that "a future unimagined cannot be achieved" or as Steven Covey so elegantly stated: A core habit of the highly successful, a condition to which we all strive, is "To begin with the end in mind."

NOTES

1. "The 21st century will be the century of the social sector organization. The more economy, money, and information become global, the more community will matter. And only the social sector nonprofit organization performs in the community, exploits its opportunities, mobilizes its local resources, [and] solves its problems. The leadership, competence, and management of the social sector nonprofit organization will thus largely determine the values, the vision, the cohesion, and the performance of the 21st century society." See The Leader to Leader Institute (formerly *The Drucker Foundation*), blue.isoph.com/pfdf/

2. The GPRA required that; beginning in FY 1994, there were to be among federally funded programs at least 10 three-year pilot projects in program performance goal setting, measurement, and reporting, and at least 5 two-year pilot projects in greater managerial flexibility in return for commitments to greater program performance. In 1997, the Office of Management and Budget and the General Accounting Office were to report on the results of the pilot projects. By FY 1998, the requirements of the Act for five-year strategic planning, annual program performance plans, and annual program performance reports were scheduled to come into force government-wide. For more details, see: www.conginst.org/resultsact/introduction/gprarpt.html.

3. Dr. David Hunter, Director of Evaluation, Edna McConnell, Clark Foundation, Telephone interview 8/29/02.

4. Ibid.

5. This term, "outcomes management," is gaining wide acceptance, particularly in the fields of health and human services, as a replacement for the phrase, "outcome thinking." For examples, see the University of Washington's Human Services Outcomes Management Initiative, www.washington.edu/change/proposals/humserv.html, the George Mason University College of Nursing and Health Science's Quality Improvement And Outcomes Management program, cnhs.gmu.edu/quality/, and The Annie E. Casey Foundation, Getting Results: Outcomes Management and the AECF Jobs Initiative (September 2000), www.aecf.org/jobsinitiative/outcomes_management.pdf.

6. See The Donors Forum of Chicago, "Outcome evaluation is important to an organization's clients and customers, to the philanthropic community, and to internal stakeholders because all of these parties need to know how to define and measure an organization's success."

7. Stephen R. Covey, The 7 Habits of Highly Effective People (New York: Simon and Schuster, 1989), 95-114.

8. Vikki K. Clawson, and Robert P. Bostrom and Associates. Outcome-Directed Thinking: Questions That Turn Things Around www.negia.net/~bostrom/bahome.htm, 4th Edition, 2003.

9. Jane Magruder Watkins, and Bernard J. Mohr, Appreciative Inquiry: Change at the Speed of Imagination, (San Francisco: Jossey Bass Pfeiffer; 2001).

10. Anne Warfield, Outcome Thinking: Getting Results without the Boxing Gloves, (Retrouvaille Publishing, 2000), www.augsburg.edu/pmi/articles/StacyBrandt.htm.

11. Lucy Knight, Outcome Evaluation: Three Workshops, (Evanston, Il: Knight Consulting, 2002).

12. Drucker. 1999 p. 43

13. Drucker, Peter F. Management Challenges for the 21st Century, (New York: Harper Brothers, 1999), 135-141.

14. Ibid, 136.

15. Ibid, 21.

16. A. Gabor, The Man Who Invented Quality, (New York: Times Books, 1990).

17. D. Kirkpatrick, (1959a), "Techniques for evaluating training programs," Journal for the American Society for Training and Development, 13: 3-9; D. Kirkpatrick, (1959b), "Techniques for evaluating training programs: Part 2: Learning," Journal for the American Society for Training Directors, 13: 21-26; D. Kirkpatrick, (1960a), "Techniques for evaluating training programs: Part 3: Behavior," Journal for the American Society for Training Directors, 14: 13-18; D. Kirkpatrick, (1960b), "Techniques for evaluating training programs: Part 4: Results," Journal for the American Society for Training Directors, 14: 28-32. For updated versions of Kirkpatrick's theory, see: D. Kirkpatrick, "Four Steps to Measuring Training Effectiveness," Personnel Administrator, 28,11, (1983) 19-25; D. Kirkpatrick, "Evaluating Training Programs: Evidence vs. Proof,"

Training & Development Journal, 31,11, 9-12; (1977) and D. Kirkpatrick, Evaluating Training Programs, (San Francisco, CA: Berrett-Koehler Publishers, Inc; 1994).

18. Graphic credit: Mary Bold, The Kirkpatrick Model. www.unt.edu/cpe/ module3/blk1why1.htm.

19. W.K. Kellogg Foundation, Kellogg Foundation Evaluation Handbook (Battle Creek, MI: W.K. Kellogg Foundation, 1998), 4.

20. Pamela Horst, et al, "Program Management and the Federal Evaluator," Public Administration Review, vol. 34 no.4 (1974), 300.

21. Ibid, 70.

22. Francis Heylighen, "In Memoriam Donald T. Campbell" Principia Cybernetica Web, pcp.lanl.gov/CAMPBEL.html.

23. Campbell's framework rests on three basic ideas he developed: 1) the principle of blind-variation-and selective-retention, which suggests that the processes that generate potential new knowledge are "blind," in that they do not have foresight or foreknowledge about what they will find. Out of these blind trials, however, the bad ones will be eliminated while the good ones are retained; 2) the concept of a "vicarious selector" which states that once the "correct" knowledge has been retained in memory, new trials do not need to be blind anymore, since now they will be selected internally by comparison with that knowledge, before they can undergo selection by the environment; thus, knowledge functions as a selector, vicariously anticipating the selection by the environment; 3) the organization of vicarious selectors as a "nested hierarchy," which allows the development of multilevel cognitive organization, leading to ever more intelligent and adaptive systems.

24. Marc Howard Ross, "PCIA as a Peacebuilding Tool," The Berghof Handbook for Conflict Transformation, (The Berghof Research Center for Constructive Conflict Management, July 2001), www.berghof-center.org/ handbook/ross/index.htm.

25. Claude F. Bennett, "Up the Hierarchy," Journal of Extension, Vol. XIII, no.2, 1975, 8.

26. Horst, "Program Management and the Federal Evaluator," Public Administration Review, 301.

27. Daniel Stefflebeam and William Webster, "An analysis of alternate approaches to evaluation," Evaluation Studies Review Annual, Vol. 6, 1981, 70.

28. Wholey, Joseph, Telephone interview October 17, 2002.

29. Horst, 301.

30. Bickman, L. "Functions of Program Theory," in Bickman, Len. Ed. Using Program Theory in Evaluation, (San Francisco: Jassey-Bass; 1987), 5.

31. Schwitzer, Alan M., "Using a Chain-of-Effects Framework to Meet Institutional Accountability Demands," Journal of American College Health, Jan2002, Vol. 50 Issue 4, 183, 4p. Also see A.M. Schwitzer, "Utilization-focused evaluation: Proposing a useful method of program evaluation for college counselors and student development professionals," Journal of Measurement Evaluation in Counseling and Development, 1997; 30:50-61, and A.M. Schwitzer and T. Metzinger, "Applying the Student Learning Imperative to Counseling Center Outcome Evaluation," Journal of College Student Psychotherapy, 1998;13:71-92.

32. Patton, M.Q., Utilization-focused evaluation: The new century text, (3rd ed.), (Thousand Oaks, CA. Sage; 1997).

33. Rosen, A., & E.K. Proctor, "Distinctions between treatment outcomes and their implications for treatment evaluation," Journal of Consulting and Clinical Psychology, 49, 1981, 418-425.

34. Kirkpatrick, Sharon, "The Program Logic Model: what, why and how?" Charity Village® www.charityvillage.com/charityvillage/research/rstrat3.html.

35. Taylor-Powell, Ellen, The Logic Model: a program performance framework, University of Wisconsin Cooperative Extension.

36. Kellogg Foundation, 37.

37. Kirkpatrick, op. ct.

38. MacNamara, Carter, Guidelines and Framework for Designing Basic Logic Model, www.managementhelp.org/np_progs/np_mod/org_frm.htm.

39. Taylor-Powell.

40. Ibid.

41. Ibid.

42. Micklethwait, John and Adrain Woolridge, The Witchdoctors: making sense of the management gurus (New York: Times Books, 1996), 13.

43. MacNamara.

44. Western Regional Center for the Application of Prevention Technologies www.open.org/~westcapt/ev2.htm.

45. Kansas City Kansas Public Schools, First Things First: A Framework for Successful School-Site Reform, www.kckps.k12.ks.us/documents/ftf_wp/figure1.html.
46. United Way of Milwaukee, 5.

47. Taylor-Powell.

48. Western Regional Center for the Application of Prevention Technologies.

49. Ibid, 6-7.

50. See 2GC Active Management, www.2gc.co.uk/home.asp; The Balanced Scorecard Collaborative, www.bscol.com/; and Benchmarking Plus, www.benchmarkingplus.com.au/perfmeas.htm.

51. Kaplan, Robert S. and Daniel P. Norton, The Balanced Scorecard, (Boston: Harvard Business School Press, 1996), 1.

52. Lebas, M., "Managerial Accounting in France," European Accounting Review 3, no.3 (1994), 471-487.

53. Kaplan and Norton, The Balanced Scorecard, 29.

54. Ibid, viii.

55. Benchmarking Plus, "Balanced Scorecard Performance Measurement," www.benchmarkingplus.com.au/perfmeas.htm.

56. Kaplan and Norton, 30-31.

57. Balanced Scorecard Collaborative, 1-7.

58. See Balanced Scorecard Collaborative, 7-8.

59. Kaplan and Norton, 11, Reprinted from R. Kaplan and D. Norton, "Using the Balanced Scorecard as a Strategic Management System," Harvard Business Review, (Jan-Feb 1996), 77.

60. Collins, James C. and Jerry I. Porras, Built to Last: successful habits of visionary companies, (New York: Harper Business, 1997).

61. See 2GC Active Management, www.2gc.co.uk/home.asp, for some of the latest research concerning the Scorecard's applications to public organization settings.

62. Williams, H.S., A. Webb, and W. Phillips, Outcome Funding: a new approach to targeted grantmaking, (Rensselaerville, NY: The Rensselaerville Institute; 1991), Third Edition, 45.

63. Williams, et al., 54.

64. Williams, et al., 65.

65. Ibid.

66. Ibid, 125-126.

67. Williams, et al., 140.

68. The attrition rate is represented by a "conversion factor" obtained by dividing each number by the one directly below it. For example, the conversion rate between the 2000 people aware of a program and the 400 who actually sign up is 5.0.

69. Bennett, 1975.

70. Bennett, C. & K. Rockwell, Targeting outcomes of programs (TOP): An integrated approach to planning and evaluation, Unpublished manuscript, Lincoln, NE: University of Nebraska, (1995, December).

71. Israel, Glenn, Program Development and Evaluation Center, Florida Department of Agricultural Education and Communication, www.pdec.ifas.ufl.edu.

72. Bennett, C. & K. Rockwell.

73. Knowledge gain pertains to learned information or accepted advice; it also includes comprehending economic, social, and environmental principles, and comprehending individual and group decision-making processes. Attitudes focus on individuals' beliefs, opinions, feelings, or perspectives. Skills refer to individuals' mental and physical abilities to use new or alternative practices. And, aspirations refer to ambitions, hopes, objectives, or desires. See citnews.unl.edu/TOP/english/overviewf.html

74. citnews.unl.edu/TOP/english/overviewf.html

75. General Accounting Office, Performance measurement and evaluation: Definitions and relationships, (GAO/GGD publication No. 98-26), Washington, DC: United States General Accounting Office, 1998.

76. Rockwell, Kay S., Robert J. Meduna, and Susan N. Williams, Targeting Outcomes Of Programs Help Public Policy Educators Design Evaluations, Paper for the National Public Policy Education Conference San Antonio, TX, Sept. 17, 01, available at www.farmfoundation.org/nppecindex.htm.
77. Chuck Schwabe, Deputy City Manager, City of Sunnyvale, CA, Telephone interview, May 9, 2002.

78. Mecklenburg County Board of Commissioners, M4R 164.109.58.120/departments/bocc/managing+for+results/home.asp.

79. National Governors Association, Managing for Results Overview, www.nga.org/center/managingforresults/.

80. Schwabe, Also see Maryland Department of Budget and Management, Managing For Results in Maryland State Government, www.dbm.state.md.us/html/manage4results.html.

81. Treasury Board of Canada, Managing for Results, www.tbs-sct.gc.ca/report/ govrev/00/mfr-gar_e.asp.

82. Governmental Accounting Standards Board (GASB), Concepts Statement No. 2, Service Efforts and Accomplishments Reporting, (Norwalk, CT: GASB, April 1994).

83. Other performance measurement standards also exist, such as the use of service quality indicators, which focus on customer satisfaction, timeliness, and accuracy and workload or demand measures.

84. Public Library Association, Training Resources for Managing for Results: Effective Resource Allocation for Public Libraries, www.pla.org/conference/managing.html.

85. The Lewin Group, The Outcome of Outcomes Research at AHCPR: Final Report. www.ahcpr.gov/clinic/outcosum.htm, New Zealand State Services Commission, Workshop 1: About Outcomes and State Indicators - Proceedings, www.ssc.govt.nz/display/document.asp?DocID=2539.

86. The entire Getting to Outcomes Training Series is accessible online in CSAP's Decision Support System at www.preventiondss.org.

87. Matthew Chinman, Pamela Imm, Abraham Wandersman, Shakeh Kaftarian, Jim Neal, Karen T. Pendleton, Chris Ringwalt, "Using the Getting to Outcomes (GTO) Model in a Statewide Prevention Initiative," Health Promotion Practice Oct 2001;2 (4) Supp 277.

88. Center for Substance Abuse Prevention, 1999 Pilot Training Manual, Getting to Outcomes: Methods and Tools for Planning, Self-Evaluation and Accountability.

89. Ibid, 3.

90. State of Maine, State Planning Office, www.state.me.us/spo/stratpla/ initiative/sporeview/guidelines.htm.

91. ncth.confex.com/ncth/2002/techprogram/paper_6470.htm.

92. American Therapeutic Recreation Association, www.atra-tr.org/ midyear/2001/pre.htm

93. University of Wisconsin Extension, Evaluation Logic Model Evaluation Bibliography, www.uwex.edu/ces/pdande/evaluation/ evallogicbiblio.html, Baptist Community Ministries, Evaluation and Research, www.bcm.org/resources.htm.

94. Scales and Ladders Committee, CSBG Monitoring and Assessment Task Force, Scales, From A to Y: Everything You Ever Wanted to Know…but Were Afraid to Ask, September, 1999, For further information see www.roma1.org/../committees/scales.html.

95. Examples of categories and their particular indicators may be found at www.csd.ca.gov/03CSBGForms.html.

96. Scales and Ladders Committee.

97. Tennessee Department of Human Services and The University of Tennessee College of Social Work, Office of Research and Social, The Guide to Implementing ROMA for CSBG Agencies in Tennessee, January 2000, 5.

98. ICCS, Matrix Evaluation Model, iccs.csumb.edu/html /community/matrix/cs11.htm.

99. Pacific Institute for Research and Evaluation, 1229 E. Franklin St. 2nd Fl. Chapel Hill, NC 27514, www.pire.org/resultmapping/First%20page.htm and www.pire.org/categories/PE.asp.

Outcome Frameworks

100. Ibid, 16.

101. Friedman, however, also credits several institutional sponsors and a number of contributing and advice authors. See Mark Friedman, The Results and Performance Accountability Implementation Guide: questions and answers about how to do the work, March, 2001 version, www.raguide.org.

102. www.resultsaccountability.com.

103. © Copyright Mark Friedman, FPSI, 2000, 2001, 2002, www.raguide.org/crosswalk_blank.htm.
104. Friedman, 2001.
105. For a discussion of the experience of the workforce field see Robert Barnow, Johns Hopkins University. Is the New Obsession With Performance Management Masking the Truth About Social Programs? With Ann B. Blalock. www.rockinst.org/publications/federalism/QuickerBetterCheaperChapter17.pdf; Barnow, Burt S. 1999. *Exploring the Relationship Between Performance Management and Program Impact: A Case Study of the Job Training Partnership Act.* Baltimore, MD: Institute for Policy Studies, Johns Hopkins University; *Publicly Funded Training in a Changing Labor Market.* Burt S. Barnow and Christopher T. King @ www.urban.org/pubs/improving/ chapter1.html; *Improving the Odds: Increasing the Effectiveness of Publicly Funded Training* (1999). Christopher T. King and Burt Barnow, eds. Washington, D.C.: Urban Institute Press. (Available from Urban Institute Press, 1-877-UIPRESS.); Barnow, B. (1986, February). The impact of CETA programs on earnings: A review of the literature. *Journal of Human Resources*, 22: 157-193; Loprest, Pamela J., and Burt S. Barnow. October 1993. Estimating the Universe of Eligibles for Selected ETA Programs. Prepared for the U.S. Department of Labor.

SELECTED BIBLIOGRAPHY

Administration on Aging. (2000) Performance outcomes measures project. Washington, D.C. Author.

Administration on Aging. Performance outcomes Measures project: Project overview. <http://www.gpra.net/>.

Alkin, M.C. "Evaluation Theory Development." Evaluating action programs. Ed. Carol Weiss. Boston: Allyn and Bacon, 1972. 115.

Balanced Scorecard Collaborative. (2001). Building the Balanced Scorecard: practitioner's guidebook. Author.

Bennett, C.F. "Up the Hierarchy." Journal of Extension. 7.2 (1975): 8.

Bennett, C. & Rockwell. Targeting outcomes of programs (TOP): An integrated approach to planning and evaluation. Unpublished manuscript. Lincoln, NE: University of Nebraska. 1995.

Bickman, L. Ed. Using program theory in evaluation. San Francisco: Jassey-Bass; 1987.

Bickman, L. Validity and social experimentation: Donald Campbell's legacy. Thousand Oaks, CA: Sage Publications; 2000.

Birdi, K.. "What is training evaluation?" University of Sheffield Institute of Work Psychology. <http://www.shef.ac.uk/~iwp/publications/whatis/training_eval.pdf..>

Campbell D. & J. Stanley. Experimental and quasi-experimental designs for research. New York: Houghton Mifflin College; 1966. Currently published by Houghton Mifflin with co-authors Thomas D. Cook and William Shadish, and available in a 2001, 2nd edition.

Center for Substance Abuse Prevention. (1999) Pilot training manual. Getting to outcomes: Methods and tools for planning, self-evaluation and accountability. Author.

Chinman, M.., et al. "Using the Getting to Outcomes model in a statewide prevention initiative." Health Promotion Practice. 2.4 (2001):Supp 277.

Ciocco, Antonio. "On indices for the appraisal of Health Department activities." Journal of Chronic Diseases. 11 (1960): 509-522.

Clawson, V.K. & R. P. Bostrom. Outcome-directed thinking: Questions that turn things around 4th Edition. Athens, GA: Bostrom and Associates. 2003. <http://www.negia.net/ ~bostrom/bahome.htm>.

Covey, S.R. The 7 habits of highly effective people. New York: Simon and Schuster; 1989.

Drucker, Peter. Managing the nonprofit organization. New York: Harper Collins; 1990.

--- Management challenges for the 21st century. New York: Harper Brothers, 1999.

Fleschut, K., Caldwell, C. & B.E. Beyt, Jr. "Managing and redesigning the continuum of care: The value chain model." Quality Management in Health Care. 5.1 (1996).

Foster, S.L. & E.J. Marsh. "Assessing Social Validity in Clinical Treatment Research Issues and Procedures" Journal of Consulting and Clinical Psychology. 67.3 (1999): 308-319.

Friedman, Mark. The results and performance accountability implementation guide: Questions and answers about how to do the work. March 2001. < http://www.raguide.org/>

Gabor, A. The man who invented quality. New York: Times Books; 1990.

General Accounting Office. Performance measurement and evaluation: Definitions and relationships (GAO/GGD publication No. 98-26). Washington, DC: United States General Accounting Office. 1998. Author.

George, S. & A..Weimerskirch. Total quality management. New York: Wiley & Sons; 1994.

Giloth, R. & W. Phillips. Getting results: Outcomes management and the Annie E. Casey Foundation's jobs initiative. Rensselaerville, N.Y.: The Rensselaerville Institute; 2000.

Governmental Accounting Standards Board. Concepts statement no. 2: Service efforts and accomplishments reporting. Norwalk, CT: GASB, April 1994. Author.

Horst, P., et al. "Program management and the federal evaluator." Public Administration Review vol. 34.4 (1974): 300.

Johnson, N. "The future of outcomes management: Views from thought leaders in the field." Formulary. 34.9 (1999): 776.

Kaplan, R. S. & D. P. Norton. The Balanced Scorecard. Boston: Harvard Business School Press; 1996.

--- "Using the Balanced Scorecard as a strategic management system." Harvard Business Review. 74(1) (1996): 77.

Kibel, Barry. Success stories as hard data.. New York: Plenum Publications; 1999. Abridged version available at <http://www.pire.org/resultmapping/abridge.htm>

Kirkpatrick, D. "Techniques for evaluating training programs." Journal for the American Society for Training and Development.13 (1959): 3-9

--- "Techniques for evaluating training programs: Part 2: Learning." Journal for the American Society for Training Directors.13 (1959): 21-26.

--- "Techniques for evaluating training programs: Part 3: Behavior." Journal for the American Society for Training Directors 14 (1960): 13-18.

--- "Techniques for evaluating training programs: Part 4: Results." Journal for the American Society for Training Directors. 14 (1960): 28-32.

--- "Evaluating training programs: Evidence vs. proof." Training & Development Journal. 31.11 (1977): 9-12.

---- "Four steps to measuring training effectiveness." Personnel Administrator, 28.19 (1983): 25.

--- Evaluating Training Programs. San Francisco, CA: Berrett-Koehler Publishers, Inc;1994.

Knight, Lucy. Outcome evaluation: Three workshops. Evanston, Il: Knight Consulting, 2002.

Knutson, Andie. "Evaluation program progress." Public Health Reports, 70 (1955) 305-310.

Lebas, M. "Managerial accounting in France." European Accounting Review 3.3 (1994): 471-487

Micklethwait, John and Woolridge, Adrain. The Witchdoctors: making sense of the management gurus. New York: Times Books; 1996.

Maljanian, R. (1999) "Building an integrated hospital-based outcomes research program." Medical Outcomes Trust Monitor 4(1).

Mullen, Edward J. "Evidence-based social work - Theory & Practice: Historical and reflective perspective." Fourth International Conference on Evaluation for Practice. University of Tampere, Tampere, Finland July 4-6, 2002.

Patton, M.Q. Utilization-focused evaluation: The new century text. 3rd ed. Thousand Oaks, CA. Sage; 1997.

Porter, M.E. Competitive advantage: Creating and sustaining superior performance. New York: Simon & Schuster Adult Publishing Group; 1985.

Preston, T. "Gaining through training: Developing high performing policy advisors." Working Paper No. 2. The New Zealand State Services Commission. September 1999.

Rayport, J & J. Sviokla. "Exploring the Virtual Value Chain" Harvard Business Review 73.6 (1995) 141-150.

Rockwell, S. K., R. J. Meduna & S.N. Williams. Targeting outcomes of programs helps public policy educators design evaluations. Paper for the National Public Policy Education Conf. San Antonio, TX . 17 September 2001. <http://www.farmfoundation.org/nppecindex.htm>.

Rosen, A. & E.K. Proctor. "Distinctions between treatment outcomes and their implications for treatment evaluation." Journal of Consulting and Clinical Psychology, 49 (1981): 418-425.

Ross, M.H. "PCIA as a peacebuilding tool." The Berghof handbook for conflict transformation. The Berghof Research Center for Constructive Conflict Management, July 2001.

Scales and Ladders Committee, CSBG Monitoring and Assessment Task Force. Scales, From A to Y: Everything You Ever Wanted to Know…but Were Afraid to Ask September, 1999. Author.

Schwitzer, A.M. "Utilization-focused evaluation: Proposing a useful method of program evaluation for college counselors and student development professionals." Journal of Measurement Evaluation in Counseling and Development. 30 (1997): 50-61.

--- "Using a Chain-of-Effects framework to meet institutional accountability demands." Journal of American College Health. 50.4 (2002):183.

Schwitzer A.M. & T. Metzinger. "Applying the student learning imperative to counseling center outcome evaluation." Journal of College Student Psychotherapy. 13 (1998): 71-92.

Spath, P.L., ed. Medical effectiveness and outcomes management. San Francisco: Jassey-Bass;1996.

Stefflebeam, D. & W. Webster. "An analysis of alternate approaches to evaluation." Evaluation Studies Review Annual. Vol. 6, 1981.

Syndenstricker, E.. "The measurement of results in public health work." Annual Report of the Milbank Memorial Fund. New York; 1926.

Taylor-Powell, E. The Logic Model: a program performance framework. University of Wisconsin Cooperative Extension <http://www2.uta.edu/sswgrants/Technical%20Assistance/ Logic_Model_presentation.pdf>

Tennessee Department of Human Services and the University of Tennessee College of Social Work, Office of Research and Public Service. The guide to implementing ROMA for CSBG agencies in Tennessee. January 2000. Author.

United States Department of Health and Human Services. Community scales: A ladder to the Twenty First Century. Washington ,D.C.: Office of Community Services, 1997. Author.

United Way of America. Measuring program outcomes: a practical approach. Arlington, VA: United Way of America; 1996. Author.

United Way of Greater Milwaukee. Lessons Learned III: using outcome data. Milwaukee, WI: United Way of Greater Milwaukee; 1998. Author.

W.K Kellogg Foundation. W.K. Kellogg Foundation evaluation handbook. Battle Creek, MI: The W.K. Kellogg Foundation; 1998. Author.

Warfield, A. Outcome Thinking: Getting results without the boxing gloves. Retrouvaille Publishing, 2000.

Weiss, C. Evaluating action programs. Boston: Allyn and Bacon, 1972.

--- Evaluation Research: methods for assessing program effectiveness. Englewood Cliffs, NJ: Prentice-Hall; 1972

Weiss, C. ed. Using social research in public policy-making. (Lexington, MA: Lexington Books; 1977).

Williams, H.S., A. Webb and W. Phillips. Outcome Funding: A New Approach to Targeted Grantmaking. 3rd ed. Rensselaerville, NY: The Rensselaerville Institute; 1991.

World Bank Environment Department. Environmental performance indicators: A first edition note. Washington, D.C.: The World Bank; 1996. Author.

ABOUT THE AUTHORS

Robert M. Penna, lead author of <u>Outcome</u> <u>Frameworks</u>, is Senior Consultant with the Rensselaerville Institute. In addition to his significant contributions to this publication, he has consulted for the Institute with the Annie E. Casey Foundation, the National Geographic Foundation, the Ford Foundation, and the United Nations. Prior to joining the Institute, Dr. Penna served for fourteen years on the staff of the New York State legislature in a variety of policy and research positions. He is a graduate of Fordham University and holds a Ph.D. in Political Science from Boston University with a specialization in urban and municipal affairs.

William J. Phillips is Vice President of The Rensselaerville Institute and Director of its Center for Outcomes. The Center's "Think Tank" perspective is manifested through prototype projects, seminars, workshops, research and publications on outcome related topics. During the past 15 years, Mr. Phillips has played a key role in the Institute's development as a recognized leader in the creation of community and organizational results for government, non profit groups and philanthropy. His consultation practice of several hundred engagements and has been both national and international in scope and includes projects in the United Kingdom, Canada and with the United Nations. He co-authored <u>Outcome Funding-a New Approach to Targeted Grant-making</u> and has authored a range of articles and case studies on outcome topics. Prior to joining the Institute, Mr. Phillips served in senior management positions in state government. He holds a BA in sociology and a Masters in Social Welfare from the University at Albany, in New York.